THE BLOODY NORTH
INFAMOUS ULSTER MURDER CASES

Born in Derry, where he still lives, Sean McMahon was educated at St Columb's College and Queen's University, Belfast. Well known as a critic, writer and editor, he is the author of *A Short History of Ireland, A Short History of Ulster* and *The History of County Derry*, as well as brief lives of Wolfe Tone, Charles Stewart Parnell, Daniel O'Connell and Tom Moore. He has also written full length biographies of Sam Hanna Bell and Robert Lynd. In addition, Sean has compiled such anthologies as *Rich and Rare, The Derry Anthology, The Poolbeg Book of Children's Verse, Taisce Duan* and, with Jo O'Donoghue, *The Mercier Companion to Irish Literature* and *Brewer's Dictionary of Irish Phrase and Fable*.

THE BLOODY NORTH

INFAMOUS ULSTER MURDER CASES

Sean McMahon

THE BREHON PRESS
BELFAST

First published 2007 by The Brehon Press Ltd
1A Bryson Street, Belfast BT5 4ES, Northern Ireland

© 2007 Sean McMahon

The right of Sean McMahon to be identified as the author of this work
has been asserted by him in accordance with the
Copyright, Designs and Patents Act 1988.

All rights reserved. No part of this publication may be
reproduced or utilised in any form or by any means digital,
electronic or mechanical including photography, filming,
video recording, photocopying, or by any information storage
and retrieval system or shall not, by way of trade or
otherwise, be lent, resold or otherwise circulated in any form
of binding or cover other than that in which it is published
without prior permission in writing from the publisher.

ISBN: 978 1905474 14 1

Design: December Publications
Printed and bound by JH Haynes and Co Ltd, Sparkford

CONTENTS

Introduction	7
Chapter 1: Mary Anne Knox	9
Chapter 2: Charlotte Hinds	25
Chapter 3: James Murray	41
Chapter 4: William Glass	49
Chapter 5: The Third Earl of Leitrim	65
Chapter 6: Nora and Arthur	81
Chapter 7: Conell Boyle	105
Chapter 8: John Flanagan	119
Chapter 9: William Barber	135
Chapter 10: Jennie Fox/Cissie Moffat	145
Chapter 11: Jennie McClintock, William McClintock and Helen Mackworth	159
Chapter 12: Mary McGowan	171
Chapter 13: Patricia Curran	193
Chapter 14: Penny McAllister	209
Select Bibliography	221

To Maeve and Brian

INTRODUCTION

It is a truth often stated that murder never fails to fascinate. The detective story, as written by Arthur Conan Doyle, Agatha Christie, and thousands of others, has sanitised the act and made it almost cosy. People who might faint at the sight of blood still consider it a pleasure to settle down with a good whodunit. Real murder is not pleasant; though, infrequently, one can, given a knowledge of all the facts, have some sympathy with the perpetrator, but it remains a bloody deed.

The deed fascinates us because of its finality; many people with no belief in an afterlife understand only its total extinction of what constitutes the person. Life is all there is and the snuffing out of it the worst possible thing that one human can do to another. Murder is also a classless sort of crime—it has been done by all classes and conditions of men from dukes to down-and-outs. Many who would have shuddered at the thought of theft or highway robbery have found it in themselves to commit this most absolute of crimes. 'Thou shalt not kill' was a very significant item on the list given to Moses on Sinai.

Considering the history of Ulster for the last forty years it may seem odd to look for stories of violent death. This book does not consider any of the killings associated with our recent Troubles; the cases described are mainly of private practice, with no overt political aspects to them. An exception might be made of the account of the death of William Clements, the Third Earl of Leitrim. Its interest lies in the consideration of what makes murder happen. Observers from outside our country might smile at protests of general lawfulness here but it is a fact that—the excesses of armed struggles aside—Ireland had, until the recent burgeoning of drug-related felonry and the knife culture, an enviable record of virtual crimelessness. Even here, however, murder makes its own rules. In the Sherlock Holmes story *The Copper Beeches* the great detective observes to his patient colleague, 'It is my belief, Watson, founded upon my experience, the lowest and vilest alleys of London do not present a more dreadful record of sin than does the smiling and beautiful countryside.' One could with some truth insert Ulster as the second last word in Doyle's sentence. He had been a practising doctor before becoming a famous writer and knew that there is no soil in which murder will not grow.

The spurs to killing are universal: rage, greed, lust, covetousness, envy, even pride—in fact all the seven deadly sins except sloth. Another potent stimulus to murder is fear, of discovery, of repetitive blackmail, of violence, and Ulster is no exception. Icon interpreters might say that the province's symbol, the hand used to claim ownership, covered with blood, suggests a bloody precedent. *The Bloody North* describes killings from different eras and includes a variety of victims and motives.

I take this opportunity of thanking those who were generous with time, help and advice: the staff of the Linen Hall Library of Belfast, especially John Killen; the staff of the Central Library in Derry, especially Jane Nicholas and Gerry Quinn; Danny Heraghty, Brian McMahon, Maeve Breslin and particularly the Derry historian, Ken McCormack.

1
MARY ANNE KNOX

Prehen House lies about one and a half miles from Craigavon Bridge on the east bank of the Foyle. When it was built in 1745 there was no bridge across the river and those who had business on the west bank where the walled city was set had to go by ferry. The house was designed by the fashionable Derry architect, Michael Priestley, who was also responsible the following year for the Lifford Court House and Port Hall, a fine house on the Lifford–Derry road. Prehen Estate, once 3,641 acres, had been the home of the Tomkins family since the middle of the seventeenth century. The name comes from the Irish word *préachán*, meaning 'crow' and with all the carefully planted trees it was a fine example of what that notable murderer Macbeth called a 'rooky wood'. It was built by Andrew Tomkins, the local landlord, and on his daughter Honoria's marriage to one of the Knoxes of Moneymore and Rathmullan, it reverted to the Knox family, which would in time produce a few bishops, an editor of *Punch* magazine, a cracker of the Enigma code during WW1 and a convert to Catholicism who produced a modern translation of the Bible.

Mary Anne Knox was born in Prehen to Honoria and husband Andrew, who was member for Donegal in the Irish parliament, in 1740. The new house may have been a gift for the distinguished son-in-law and only daughter. It would be inherited by Mary, who, according to a contemporary document, printed in London in 1762, is described in maturity as

> ...of a middling stature, and very elegantly formed, her hair was light, with an agreeable tendency to the golden

hue, serving only to enliven her complexion, which nothing could exceed; her features were extreamly regular, and there was a mixture of the tender and the sprightly in her countenance which is seldom seen; it was indeed expressive of that mildness and affability, which so eminently distinguished her character.

The note on the title page states that the account was

compiled from Papers communicated by a Gentleman in Ireland, to a Person of Distinction of that Kingdom, now residing here.

The story of Prehen House and the death of the elegant heiress have fascinated the people of Ulster for nearly 250 years. The coach in which Mary Anne was killed was on show in the old museum in Derry. Schoolboy stories of the coach regularly filling up with blood were accepted if never proved. The beautifully refurbished four-wheeled carriage, fitted with the latest springing and twin lanterns coach, is now on display in the Tower Museum in the city. It was known to contemporaries as a 'travelling chariot' and was probably as impressive as a modern Lexus or even a Rolls-Royce — such was perfectly appropriate for a gentleman of Andrew Knox's position. Mary Anne was an heiress in her own right. She had £6,000 pounds by the marriage settlement of her parents and should her older brother die without issue she would have an annual income of £1,500. (These amounts should be multiplied by at least a thousand to give some idea of their modern equivalence.)

The mid-eighteenth century in Ireland was relatively peaceful, until the rising of 1798. The Catholic Irish had been rendered quiescent by the virtual loss of their upper classes, who had fled the country as 'wild geese', and through penal laws preventing their owning land or obtaining an education. The majority lived lives of silence; it was essentially a Protestant century in which the Anglo-Irish were — with rare exceptions —

the only people who mattered. It meant that the ascendancy class were the Irish nation. The parliament of which Andrew Knox was a member had little power and was essentially a somnolent creature of Westminster. This would change with the American War of Independence and the coming of the Irish Volunteers but during the short life of Mary Anne Knox the country was insurrection free and formally peaceful — though not crime free. It was the golden age of the highwaymen, those ironically named 'gentlemen of the road' who made travel perilous. In the few cities those who could afford them moved around after dark with 'linkmen', boys carrying torches, and armed bodyguards were needed to protect wayfarers against vicious gangs who roamed the streets. In the countryside there were local watchmen, who acted as borough constables, but they had little power and usually less courage.

A serious danger for young heiresses was the adventurer. These men worked upon the finer feelings of these vulnerable women, happily marrying them if there was no other way of separating them from their wealth. Later in the century a number of abduction clubs were formed in Dublin. Its members found it financially advantageous to supply adventurers with possible partners, circumventing the tedious formalities of courtship and betrothal by direct action. In a small quiet city like Londonderry, one with a reputation for Puritanism, adventurers worked singly and used charm rather than violence. Mary Anne's nemesis was one such in the person of John McNaghten from Benvarden in County Antrim.

John was born in either 1722 or 1724, a scion of a Scottish family that arrived at Carrickfergus with William III in 1688. The Benvarden Estate netted about £500 a year and earlier generations had played their part in public service. His father and uncle had been magistrates, the latter later defending the country with the Antrim militia from the opportunistic foray of the French captain Louis Thurot, who took Carrickfergus during the Seven Years War. He was educated at the Royal School,

Raphoe, in County Donegal and at Trinity, where the addiction to gambling that was to ruin his life showed itself. Having come of age he gambled away his inheritance and left without taking a degree. While he was at Raphoe he gained a reputation for quarrelling and also for cowardice. When he was eighteen he had a row with a schoolmate who challenged him to a duel. The challenger arrived but had brought not a sword but a whip. McNaghten was given a thorough thrashing and ran away — something that would haunt him for the rest of his life. Eighteenth-century public schools were not for the faint-hearted.

Whatever about his short temper he must have had more than his share of charm — at least with women. His uncle so disapproved of his addiction to 'play' — as gambling for high stakes was known — that he cut him out of his will, forcing the adventurer-to-be to scratch a living. He sold some of the Benvarden Estate and mortgaged the rest. Meanwhile, the Earl of Massereene, one of the largest landowners in South Antrim, introduced John to his sister-in-law Miss Daniel. They decided to marry with the condition that he would never again 'play'. He seems to have been a loving husband but the strength of his addiction was such that he persuaded himself that the oath was no longer binding. He was an unlucky gambler since he never seemed to win. As a result he owed money to many creditors who proceeded against him with writs. On one occasion the sheriff's officers determined to execute their writs discovered where he was 'playing' and surrounded the house. He stayed very late and escaped in a sedan chair which the officers had no power to stop. They followed him home, however, and sought to arrest him but he resisted. His heavily pregnant wife was so shocked by the disturbance and the realisation of the extent of his debts that she collapsed and died. As our Gentleman in Ireland put it:

> The noise first alarmed her, and upon hearing the occasion of it, she was so terrified at the apprehensions of his

MARY ANNE KNOX

> danger, and so shocked at the desperate situation of his affairs, that she fell into a nervous disorder, which, in a very short time, put an end to her life.

The tragedy had a sobering effect upon him as he was genuinely fond of his wife at a time and in a class when marriages were largely business contracts. He tried to overcome his misfortunes 'in a perpetual succession of gay company and the fascinating power of play'. In the society in which he moved his kind of recklessness was not uncommon or strongly criticised. He had lost none of his charm and was able to persuade his brother-in-law to be one of the sureties for a bond of £2,000. His old friend Lord Massereene did not forsake him, obtaining for him the position of collector of taxes ('the King's duty') for the county of Coleraine, as County Derry was once called. Even this he squandered and in less than two years, with £800 of the King's money unaccounted for, he lost the position and his bondsmen were held liable for the debt. Still his luck held when Andrew Knox MP, who knew the McNaghten family, offered him the hospitality of Prehen.

He made good use of it, spending his time between Strabane, Coleraine, Benvarden and Derry. He was in permanent danger of arrest for peculation and unpaid debts yet stood as member for Coleraine, 'without the least interest or probability of success' but merely as a means of obtaining more credit. He failed there but stood for Derry 'with the same view, and with the same success'. It was time to turn his attention to his host's daughter Mary Anne. He targeted the lady herself, who was his junior by sixteen years, and became a frequent guest at Prehen. It was an elegant house with substantial grounds and fine views of the upper Foyle and would, one day, belong to Mary Anne.

The eighteenth century was different from the one that followed. It was altogether freer and more *louche*. In the quasi-aristocratic circles fifteen years of age was not regarded as immature. In Prehen, as the only daughter, Mary Anne would have been expected to act as hostess, well-drilled in these duties by Honoria.

There is no reason to suppose that he was not fond of the girl but his purpose was largely mercenary. She was not averse to his attentions but as a seasoned campaigner John knew that Andrew Knox was an important part of the equation. However, when he approached his host, it became clear that whatever friendship and hospitality he had received, McNaghten's reputation was such that there could be no question of an alliance. McNaghten rather cleverly made no complaint but rather entreated Andrew to keep his proposal a secret, even from other members of the family. Mary Anne was aware that her lover had talked to her father and was not too distressed at his reaction. She probably regarded it as the first action in a long campaign. The parents continued their kindness to their guest. Honoria had several times remarked to her daughter that 'she should be glad of so pretty a fellow for a son-in-law'.

McNaghten's next move had a wicked ingenuity about it. He persuaded Mary Anne to read with him the words of the marriage ceremony. This they did at the house of Joshua Swetenham in Derry. They made a solemn reading of the service in the presence of seventeen-year-old Andrew Hamilton. McNaghten prevailed upon her to kiss the book with him and made her solemnly swear that she should be married to him by a clergyman at the first opportunity. She was, however, not so enamoured of him that she neglected to add 'provided her father would consent'. This was a setback but he continued to persuade her that what had passed between them was a genuine marriage contract, the awkward bit about her father's consent having come after the solemnisation. He then embarked on the oldest ploy in the game. He determined to seduce her and, if she should become pregnant, the campaign would have been won.

An opportunity presented itself when he was asked to escort Mary Anne on a journey to visit friends, the Wrays, at Ards in County Donegal. They spent the first night in Strabane in the house of John McCausland and the dashing squire hoped there to complete the second part of his campaign. If Mary Anne could be made pregnant her parents would have no further objections to the suit. However, Mrs McCausland spiked his plan. Whether she had warning from Prehen or decided that something about McNaghten was suspicious she had Mary Anne sleep in her dressing room. Presumably the thwarted villain spent the night in a rage of frustration. Next morning, in the McCausland garden, he attempted to have his foul way with Mary Anne. She repulsed his advances with great firmness and disappointment, and ran back to the house. His actions horrified her and she determined to continue her journey without him.

She was badly hurt and shocked by her experience and Angel Wray, her coeval and close friend, couldn't help but notice the change. She was anxious to discover the reason for her friend's unusual mood and finally persuaded her to say what was wrong. Mary Anne told her of McNaghten's addresses to her and of her previous tenderness towards him. She further described the mock marriage ceremony in Derry and what had happened in the garden. Angel Wray immediately told her father who sent Mary Anne back to Prehen, properly attended, in case the villain should still be in the district. His letter to Andrew Knox made fairly plain his reasons for her return. McNaghten, however, was not finished yet. He insisted that he had married Mary Anne and placed a piece in the newspapers to say that they had been legally wed. The public prints, as they were called, became a battleground when Andrew Knox contradicted McNaghten's account with his own press notices. These advertisements grew steadily more strident and menacing, giving the gossips the best story for years.

At this point McNaghten was living in Derry, at the home of his mother's brother, Charles MacManus. John narrated his version of events to his indulgent uncle. When they heard that Mary Anne had been removed for safety to the home of her uncle James Knox in Sligo uncle and nephew headed there.

McNaghten persisted in his determination to prove that Mary Anne was his wife, ignoring public insults with an unbelievable insouciance. An assembly, an eighteenth-century combination of dancing, music and social intercourse, was announced for the town and McNaghten made his way there, hoping that Mary Anne might attend. Her cousin, Thomas, James's son, was at the assembly with his friend, John MacGill, member for Rathcormack in County Cork and commissioner of the Board of Works. MacGill, incensed at the injuries done to the Knox family, said in a whisper loud enough for those standing near, that McNaghten was 'a very great scoundrel' but John did not react. He returned to his uncle who also had a house in Sligo. As the night wore on, the company, including a certain Lieutenant Gethings, persuaded him that such a gross and public insult should be answered by a challenge. In the Ireland of the time duelling was a common way of achieving 'satisfaction'. Gethings offered himself as a second and brought the challenge to MacGill at his inn. *He* readily accepted and arranged for a second.

It was a bright May morning when they met. Neither party had slept and with the discharge of the first pistols both missed. At the second attempt McNaghten missed again but was wounded in the left ankle, the ball passing through the Achilles tendon and the bone. The ever optimistic and self-deluding McNaghten assumed that his taking part in a duel removed all slurs on his character. He tried his famous charm on MacGill, hoping that 'he did not now think him so great a scoundrel, as he had declared he thought him in the assembly-room'. MacGill was not mollified and answered, 'By God, but I do.' In spite of this the wounded gentleman made a slow but triumphal journey by Donegal and Ballybofey to Derry, being carried by litter with his wound of honour, suffered in a duel about a young lady, prominently displayed. In those days news travelled slowly and few people were able to read, much less afford the public papers. To a majority of ordinary inhabitants of the northeast corner of

Ireland he was clearly a gentleman and a gallant one besides.

For some months he continued in his usual career of sponging successfully off gullible patrons and blowing any money garnered at the gaming tables. He found it judicious to spend some time out of Ireland, fearing that a bench warrant obtained by Andrew Knox might be processed. Ever ambitious he sought among minor English aristocracy for a sponsor who might support him in an election for the seat of Carrickfergus. Like all his schemes this came to nothing. Nevertheless he found money somewhere and was seen in Bath where he was noted as playing 'very deep' with little success. In August of 1761 he was in London where he heard that Mary Anne, along with her mother and aunt, was taking the waters in Swanlinbar, on the border of Fermanagh and Cavan. This was a popular spa, famous for its sulphur well, and was known as the 'Harrogate of Ireland'. He left immediately for Enniskillen, eight miles from the spa, making the journey in the record time of ten days.

He was still in danger of arrest and also knew that if he were recognised his quarry would be whisked away for safety so he disguised himself as a sailor

> ...with his hair cut off, and instead of it, a close white horse-hair wig, done up in buckle, such as sailors on shore generally wear, a checked shirt, and kind of loose waistcoat, tied with a rope.

He walked the eight miles in this disguise and found cheap lodging in a little hut, called a cabbin. For three days and nights, he watched the road to the spa from a wood that bordered the road. He intended to take his 'betrothed' by force. The cabbin's owner became suspicious of her lodger after she found powder and bullets tied up in the sleeve of one of his shirts and raised the alarm. McNaghten removed his disguise and with the reputation of a gentleman who had gone to such lengths to woo his love became the latest sensation in Swanlinbar. He was invited to dinner by the Bishop of Kilmore, who also was taking the waters. He became very popular with the locals, who let it be known that they would be willing 'at whatever hazard to carry off the lady'.

The more one learns about McNaghten the more one's reluctant admiration grows. He had more chutzpah than a score of Broadway producers. He made his way to Florence Court in Fermanagh, where the Knoxes had taken refuge, and asked Lord Mountflorence to let him speak to Mary Anne. His lordship agreed on condition that this would be his last interview and that he would never trouble the Knox family again. McNaghten would not accept Mountflorence's conditions and asked instead to speak to Angel Knox, Mary Anne's aunt. They met and talked for two hours but there was little in the way of dialogue — he insisted on his rights as Mary Anne's true spouse while she berated him for his persecution of the family. As he left he gave solemn assurances to Mountflorence that he would return to England directly. In fact he had no such intention; instead he resolved to grab Mary Anne. There had been many cases of such schemes and after the consummation families usually acquiesced.

For the next two months he ranged about Strabane, St Johnston, Derry, Benvarden and Inishowen, in disguise, laying his plans. In October he learned that Andrew Knox had to go to Dublin to attend to parliamentary duties. John stayed at the house of a man called Irwin which was situated on the banks of the Burndennet River, near the Dublin Road, about eight miles from Prehen. Mr Irwin's house was a common resort for gentlemen, especially of the sporting variety. One of his small band of followers told him that Knox would leave for Dublin on the morning of 10 November, taking his daughter and the rest of the family with him. He chose Cloughcor, about three miles from Strabane, as the location for the ambush. The road there was hemmed in by an oak wood and a large dunghill that, not inappropriately, would give him and his men cover. There also was a cabin there belonging to a peasant called Keys where they could hide in preparation. They took up their positions before daybreak that fateful morning. Apart from a sack, six firelocks (guns fired by a lock with flint and steel), nine pistols and several ropes, McNaghten also carried 'a long leathern strap' to tie Mary Anne behind him on his horse.

The Knox wagon train consisted of James Knox, Andrew's brother, who led the way in a single horse chaise, with a servant behind on horseback. They were followed by Mary Anne's brother with his servant, both on horseback. Then came the 'travelling chariot' with Mary Anne's parents, her body servant and the lady herself. MacCullagh, the Knox blacksmith, rode shotgun with a blunderbuss and a pair of pistols in his overcoat pocket. James Love, Andrew Knox's personal servant, brought up the rear and he was armed with a 'fusee', a kind of small eighteenth-century bazooka. In spite of all this armament security was lax. The fore-riders were not armed and had moved on too far ahead — nobody expected any attack. McNaghten and his rapparees allowed the fore party to move even further ahead and then he appeared in the middle of the road pointing his pistol at the driver of the chariot, threatening that he would shoot him if he did not stop. He ran to the left hand door, shooting MacCullagh in the hand. He aimed his blunderbuss but it misfired. The gang began to fire indiscriminately into the coach, McNaghten on the left while the others surrounded the chariot. In spite of the intensity of the fusillade only Mary Anne was hit, and it was presumed that McNaghten had fired the shot.

McNaghten and his gang disappeared while Mary Anne's brother spurred ahead to Strabane where he knew that Sir James Caldwell's regiment of Inniskilling light-horse were quartered. A doctor was fetched from Strabane for Mary Anne who had been carried into the cabin. She was bleeding heavily and complaining of excruciating pains in her side. She had been shot five times and three of the wounds were in the upper body. Dr Law, the Strabane physician, shook his head and said that she was beyond all hope of recovery. They moved her to a decent farmhouse where she died four hours later.

A party of light-horse, led by a Sergeant MacJunkin, ranged as far as Dungiven. Another party led by Sergeant Caldwell searched for McNaghten in Myroe, Limavady and Ballykelly without success. He was found in a hayloft, not far from the scene, by two members of the regiment. Fearing arrest he attempted to shoot himself in the head but the ball dropped out and he suffered no more than powder burns to his ear. The soldiers who had discharged their pistols drew their swords and seized their quarry. He was tied to a low-backed car, a kind of sledge without wheels, wearing 'an old blue lapelled coat, an old brown wig, a coarse felt hat, fustian breeches, and was without boots'. It was quite a comedown for a personable gent whose charm was legendary. He was thrown into Lifford jail to await recompense for his misdeed. His gang scattered, having the advantage of local knowledge, though one of them, a man called Dunlap, was discovered in a large meal chest at Ballybogy, about a mile and a half from Benvarden.

The inquest on Mary Anne was held on 11 November and the verdict of the inquest jury was wilful murder perpetrated by McNaghten and his accomplices. Her body was taken back to Prehen and the next day carried to Rathmullan to be buried in the Knox plot. Fearing an attempt at a rescue Andrew Knox obtained an order from the Lord Lieutenant that a guard made up of members of the light-horse should be stationed at Lifford with two unarmed soldiers sleeping in McNaghten's cell. McNaghten showed no remorse, more interested in tending to his wounds than grieving. He refused to shave and when he was brought to court in Strabane on a litter he looked very dishevelled and had a beard of a month's growth. He was as persuasive as ever, insisting that no man ever loved a woman better than he loved Miss Knox and, regarding her as his lawful wife, had arranged his ambush as the only means of securing her. The Crown witnesses swore that he had shouted to his men, 'Shoot, shoot Mary Anne.'

The trial lasted fourteen hours and he was found guilty. He bowed to the jury and commended them for their honesty; with the evidence presented they could have brought no other verdict. He pleaded the cause of Dunlap in vain, saying that he 'was a poor simple fellow, his tenant, and not intentionally guilty of any crime'. His popularity with 'the lower sort of people' was undiminished — no Strabane carpenter would build a gallows for his execution. The outraged Knoxes made the gallows themselves on the Strabane side of Lifford but when McNaghten was brought fettered from prison on 15 December 1761 no blacksmith could be found to strike off the chains, a strange legal condition at the time insisting that a man about to be hanged should have his hands free. A blacksmith was eventually compelled to remove the fetters by an officer of the light-horse, but then no hangman was available. An old man was brought from County Cavan but the bold McNaghten put the noose round his own neck. He climbed to the top of the ladder and threw himself off with great force. It should have been enough but the rope broke and he fell to the ground. He made no attempt to escape but climbed on to the platform again and this time he died.

Folk memory has him saying that he did not wish to be known as a 'half-hanged man' and that is why he preferred to finish the job. If the story is true then his dying wish was not fulfilled; he has been known as 'Half-hanged McNaghten' ever since. The rope that broke was quickly mended and used to hang poor Dunlap. The story of McNaghten and Miss Knox has been told in every generation since, sometimes presenting him as a lost romantic who dearly loved his victim. He was such a contradictory fellow that we cannot come to any conclusion. In the 1830s, when the Ordnance Survey team published their memoirs of the parish of Clondermot, they considered it important to include an account of the 'death of Miss Knox'. The event 'naturally excited much interest at the time, which length of years has but slightly abated'. The writers of the memoirs add that he was 'concealed from the officers by different females of his acquaintance [and] was discovered by some person who had observed a lady bringing food to an outhouse in which he was at the time secreted'. They also suggest that the bullets that killed Mary Anne were intended for her father. Whatever about the truth of the actual event and the nature of McNaghten's feelings towards her, the Ordnance Survey team found in the church of Killygarvan at Rathmullan a tablet in her memory which read: '*Mariana filia obiit* November 1761' ('Mary Anne, the daughter, died November 1761').

Prehen House continued to have a notable history until 1914 when its owner Baron George Carl Otto von Scheffler-Knox, a German national, returned to his other homeland. The property was confiscated by the British government who allowed it to lie empty and derelict. It still loomed heavily in the imagination of the people of Derry and the bus stop outside its impressive entrance pillars became known as the 'Black Gates'. In 1971 the house was brought back into the Knox family and lovingly restored by Julian and Carola Peck. Its former elegance recovered, it stands today as one of Derry's showpieces. Yet the story of one of its first inhabitants still haunts, and the wood at Cloughcor brings a memory of an unromantic ending to what might have been a romantic story.

2
CHARLOTTE HINDS

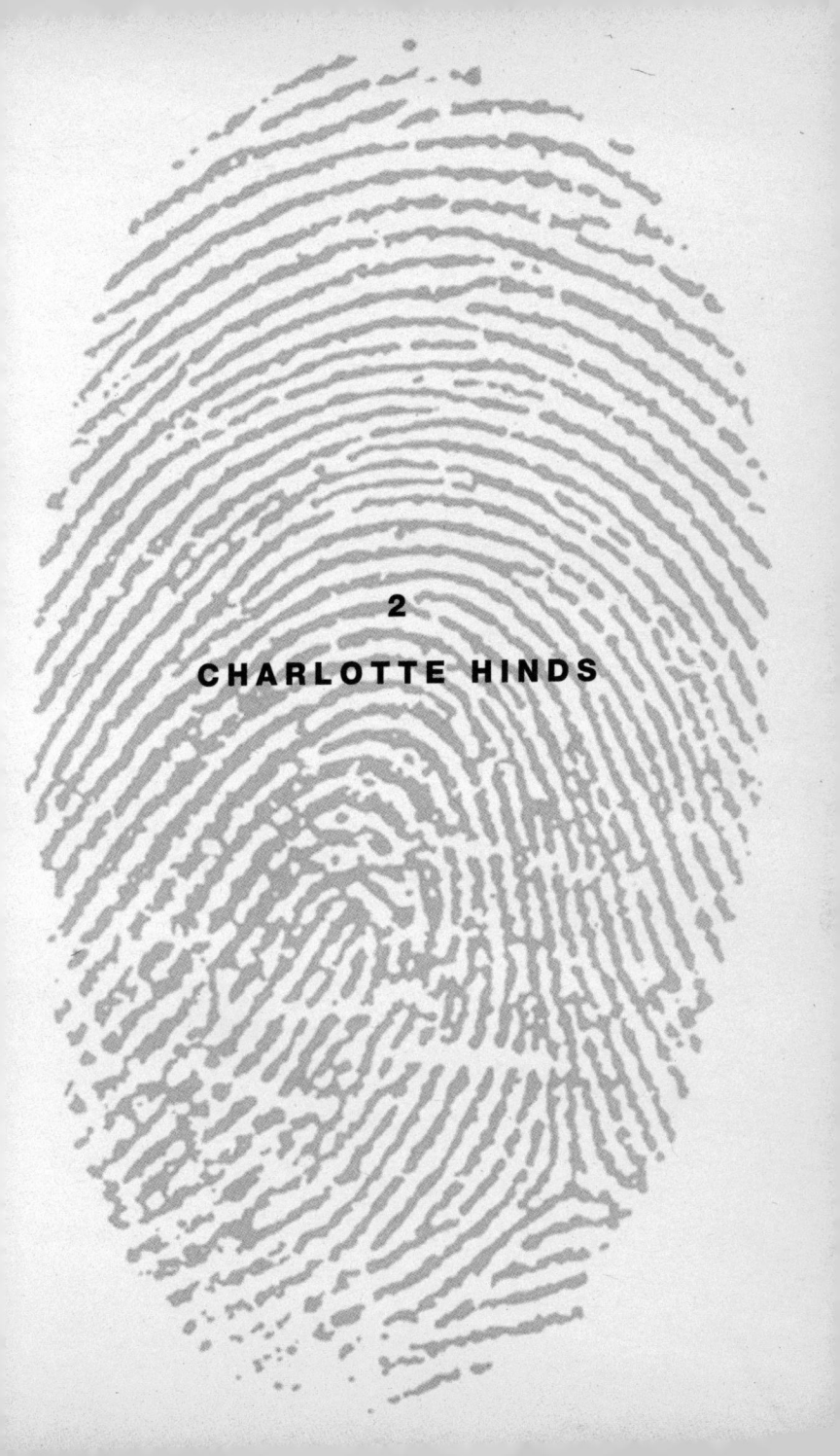

THE COUNTY OF CAVAN, with a land area of 730 square miles, is the nineteenth in size in Ireland and the fourth smallest in Ulster. Like six other Ulster counties, the exceptions being Antrim, Down and Monaghan, it was formally planted in the seventeenth century and, like all Ulster counties, its English and Scots undertakers relied on the dispossessed to help them work the land and in some cases to live as tenants on what had been the territories of native chieftains. The undertakers lived side by side with the Irish in wary peace, having as little to do with each other as possible. Two hundred and fifty years later they still eyed each suspiciously, now designated Protestants and Catholics. In fact Cavan was by the 1850s, relatively speaking, quite peaceful with some partisan cynics believing that the reason for the comparative amity was the presence of decent loyalists. The Great Famine had left its mark mainly on the tenant farmers, who were predominantly Catholic, and emigration was beginning to drain the county of its young people. The cataclysm also ruined many landlords who were unable to collect due rents during the years of the Famine, the effects of which were dire for a biblical seven years after the first appearance of the potato blight in 1845.

The years after 1815 were severely depressed economically; peace after the Napoleonic wars meant low prices for grain, and though the county avoided the social upsets of the Tithe Wars and the more extreme attentions of Carders, Houghers and Whiteboys, like a good Ulster county it had a tradition of Ribbonism. This descendant of the Defenders with its targets of

Orangemen and 'cruel' landlords was a constant worry or resource depending on your point of view. Misbehaviour of tenantry, especially regarding late payment of rent, had tended to be the rule in some areas and legitimate complaints were often met with threats, veiled or specific, of a bruising visit from Ribbonmen to the landlord's agent or the landlord himself, if he were not an absentee. By the end of the Great Hunger Ribbonism had virtually ceased to exist but there were many old adherents still alive who had passed on to their children and grandchildren the mindset and actual weapons of the heavily ritualistic secret society.

Cavan contains the source of both the Shannon and the Erne and tends to be a wet county. Alice Milligan, the Omagh poet, described it as 'Cavan of the little lakes' and its soil, like that of its eastern neighbour Monaghan, is heavy and hard to work. That county's great poet Patrick Kavanagh complained of 'the stony grey soil of Monaghan' that stole the laugh from his loving. The land in the district of Tubberlion-Diffin, a region of west Cavan where the county is squeezed between Fermanagh and Leitrim, was equally hard to work. For centuries it had belonged to the Hinds family and Ralph Hinds was one of the landowning victims of the Hungry Forties. Unpaid rents were the main cause of his financial collapse while recalcitrant tenants, plus the social and economic consequences of the Famine, added to his miseries and eventual bankruptcy. It was a fate he shared with many others of his class yet his failure rankled especially with his daughter Charlotte, who, by 1853, had recovered title to her father's lands and was determined to re-establish the family name and reputation. She left her Dublin house and, with her companion Catherine Lyng, went to live on the Hinds' land southwest of Ballyconnell.

Her intention was to make the property profitable again by collecting back rents and ensuring that the land was being worked properly. She was a determined woman and not too concerned if her rigorous regimen was seen to be cruel. Many of her tenants were cottiers who lived at virtual subsistence level. The easily grown and high-yielding 'lumper' potato required little further labour apart from sowing and harvesting. It was, however, highly susceptible to the fungus that had caused the recent cataclysm a few years ago. Work was tough at seeding and picking, and when peat had to be dug and dried in May. For the rest of the country year these peasants were idle and therefore, to the Protestant eye, feckless. Their diet of potatoes, milk and an occasional slice of bacon kept them healthy and their needs were supplied by their smallholdings. It was a lifestyle unintelligible to the outsider and had led to the belief that these tenants-at-will were a kind of sub-species, justly caricatured by *Punch* and portrayed by the *London Illustrated Journal*.

In fact they were caught in a social bind whose condition would not improve until the Irish land question was settled. The famine had begun a social revolution that the Land League, a number of Land Acts initiated by Gladstone and emigration would complete. Residual elements of Ribbonism were still to be found, with pistols and muskets hidden in the thatch, and plenty of shrubs to make cudgels — the fearful contemporary equivalent of the baseball bat. Before the setting up of the Land League in 1879 the British blamed any agrarian unrest on Ribbonism. Most of Charlotte's tenants were 'Romanists', as the unionist newspapers called them, and the Church was perceived by Ulster Protestants to be colluding with this underclass. They did not give the clergy credit for the lawlessness they prevented and judged the whole religion by the activities of the few who were not susceptible to preaching. Many of the wilder elements feared neither God nor man. Jail held no terrors for them since prison conditions were marginally better that the hovels in which they had to live. Some were driven desperate by what they saw as injustice, despite being protected by the Ulster Custom of the 'Three Fs' — fair rent, fixed tenure and free sale of holding — and were unlikely to acquiesce in the demands of a landlord, even if a woman. Their landlords ignored the deep emotions that land engendered at their peril. What the English papers saw as legitimate income the tenants interpreted as exploitation by foreigners.

Charlotte was determined to right the wrong done to her father and to collect the arrears that were due to her. Being an absentee landlord had not worked and so she became her own agent. She began to distrain for arrears of rent using eviction as the ultimate sanction. It was a sanction that caused intolerable grief to the dispossessed, falling heaviest on women and children, and was in sore contrast to the way things were under Charlotte's father. The campaign of silent menace which had broken him did not seem to bother her; death threats and damage to her property had little effect. She was not prepared to mitigate her methods in the slightest. She ignored any threats, seemingly unaware that even in modern times like the 1850s, older methods could still be used against the landlord. She does not appear to have warned the local police, the Royal Irish Constabulary (RIC), instead believing in her own invulnerability.

It was her practice to be driven to the market in Ballyconnell, which was held on the second and fourth Friday of the month. Her jaunting-car driver was a seventeen-year-old lad called James McKeon, who sat in the driving seat in control of the horse. On Friday, 12 October 1855, on the way back from the market, they picked up the elderly Andrew Reilly who was lame. He sat on the opposite side to Charlotte as the car was driven up Corrin Lane, the *casán* that led to her house. The time was between three and four in the afternoon, according to the *Dublin Evening Mail* of 15 October. McKeon got down to lead the horse because the surface of the lane was in need of repair. They had just reached Corrin Wood when two men rushed out from the trees. They were 'two demons in human shape', according to a Ballyconnell correspondent to the *Belfast News Letter*, whose letter appeared on 23 October, 'who at once dragged her off the car, knocked her down with loaded sticks, and then deliberately fired no fewer than three pistol shots into her face and head, after which they walked quietly away, leaving her for dead.'

As McKeon reported it, on hearing a scream he looked round and saw Charlotte standing in the roadway. She was being beaten about the head by the two assailants until she fell on the ground. A pistol shot caused the mare to rear and bolt and McKeon ran with it to try to quiet it down. Poor Reilly was thrown off the car and wisely disappeared into the wood. McKeon heard a second shot and perhaps a third. Charlotte did not die immediately. As another correspondent of the *News Letter* revealed:

> Miss Hinds is still alive, but her case is hopeless. She has been butchered most savagely — her leg and arm broken, and two balls lodged in her head. The doctor thought it useless to extract the balls, or set the broken limbs. She is now senseless; but shortly after the outrage she lodged informations against two of the ruffians, tenants of hers, and then feeling she had no hope of recovery, she made her will.

She managed to name one of the attackers as Red Pat Bannon, a former employee on her estate, and the other she described as 'a smart man'. It was not certain quite what she meant by 'smart' — it probably meant well-dressed, unlike the majority of the locals. The butt of a gun and a small sword were found at the scene. What Charlotte could not have known was that the perpetrators had already crossed the River Scalan in a small boat and had disappeared somewhere in the neighbouring county of Leitrim.

The local Irish Constabulary (IC) officers arrived soon after and arrested McKeon on the presumption that he was party to the attack. During questioning he showed some confusion about the details. He was uncertain about whether there were two or three men. He finally decided that two men had been present and said as much at the inquest that was held fourteen days after the attack, by which time Charlotte had succumbed. Andrew Reilly's version was different and probably more reliable since, recovered from his fall from the car, he could observe the scene from the safety of Corrin Wood. He insisted that the smart man had played no part in the attack and that Red Pat Bannon had been the assailant. His description was circulated in *Hue and Cry*, the in-house journal of the constabulary, and posters were displayed in Cavan and the neighbouring counties of Monaghan and Fermanagh to the north, Longford and Leitrim to the south. Bannon was described as five feet six inches tall, with a fair complexion, striking red hair and wearing the often caricatured frieze coat and white trousers, the standard garb of Irishmen in cartoons. Bannon was also known to have a scar on the calf of his left leg and had deserted from the Cavan Militia that year.

The Tory press seized upon the murder as a further opportunity to berate the native Irish. An article in the *Standard* was reprinted in the *Belfast News Letter,* on 1 November, since it reflected the Ulster paper's own views. There was no sympathy for, or understanding of, the social conditions that produced such desperate acts. Instead it attacked the local clergy, believing that they were in league with the 'Romanist peasantry' in refusing to give information to the authorities:

> The priest, the sink of all the crime of his parish, might pretend to the sacredness of the confessional as to any revelation made to him — sacredness which in Ireland extends to this: that the minister of religion, as religion is understood by Romanists, may not exact from his penitents to discharge their duty to man or to their Creator by denouncing criminals of whose guilt they are cognisant, though not participators in it.

The journalist showed a complete lack of awareness of the Irish psyche. The ordinary Irish peasant held one thing abhorrent with an intensity as deep as his preoccupation with having land and that was informing. Irish people were, at the time, in a state of virtual enmity with the law; how could they trust the authorities who executed the eviction orders so efficiently, destroying even the rooftrees of their hovels? The belief in the priests' ability to exact from their flocks anything other than the small stipends that provided them with their barely comfortable livings was without basis. The journalists did not really believe it themselves and the better educated among them knew how complete the seal of the confessional was. Informers were loathed and though Ribbonism was largely a spent force, its oath of silence was still powerful.

The police were not above trying to find information from the few who would risk cooperation in exchange for the reward or to get themselves off the hook. The contemporary term for a person who turned Queen's evidence was 'approver', which referred to giving proof of guilt. Initially they met with little success. The chief suspect, apart from the named Red Pat, was a close neighbour of Charlotte's called Thomas Dunne. He was part of a group of educated Catholics who were beginning to stand up for their rights. He had successfully stood for election to a local board of guardians in 1854, beating David Veitch, a local upper-class Protestant. Charlotte had personally ensured Veitch's election the following year by ordering her tenants to vote for him. Elections were open hustings then, secret ballots not being mandatory until 1872, and publicly to slight a landlord was to risk eviction. Dunne began openly to challenge Charlotte's actions; querying her methods and suggesting harshness in collecting arrears of rent that were not of very great duration. He began to gain a reputation as a successful landlord baiter and attracted the attention of Nicholas Kelly, the local RM, who after the murder, made the case his particular crusade. It was probably on his recommendation that the police initiated the new tactic of blanket arrests.

The lad McKeon had been in Cavan jail since the day of the killing and now he was joined by at least eight men, including Dunne and a Leitrim man James Murphy, who worked in

Tubberlion. The arrest of these two without obvious reason suggested that an approver was at work and it wasn't long until it was revealed who he was. Among those arrested in the IC swoop on locals was another Bannon, no relation of the most wanted Red Pat, one Terence, known locally in the north-midland accent as Black Tarry. He was described rather unflatteringly by the local paper as having a 'countenance long, meagre and pock-pitted'; his eyes were 'sunken' with shaggy eyebrows 'immediately impending over them'. The formal language of the newspapers of the time makes the description all the more unnerving.

On 9 April 1856, at a special commission at which two judges presided, Thomas Dunne and James Murphy stood trial for murder. The local authorities had insisted that the commission replace the normal assize hearing because of the serious nature of the offence and its deleterious effect on the Queen's peace in County Cavan. The commission met at Cavan courthouse before a capacity crowd, only too aware that the extra expense would be borne by the tenantry. The first witness was young McKeon, who may have been coached by Magistrate Kelly, since all his previous uncertainty had vanished. He had no difficulty in identifying Murphy as the chief assailant, the one who had first beaten Charlotte with his stick lined with lead, and then fired the shots which finally killed her. Andrew Reilly, the lame passenger, was much less certain. He recognised Red Pat but couldn't identify the other since his head was hidden by his coat. When Black Tarry began to speak it was obvious that he had turned informer. He gave damning details of a conspiracy to remove the curse of the cruel unreasonable landlord. He claimed to be the finance officer and had the task of collecting the necessary money from interested parties — or sponsorship, if you will.

He attended a meeting at Dunne's house a few nights before the murder. There he met some locals and a stranger, whom he afterwards got to know as Murphy. He said he was sent to the house of John Logan to fetch pistols and to Ballyconnell to buy powder and firing caps. He made the rounds of nearby tenants and eventually amassed almost £14, then a considerable sum of money. His role in the action was to wait on the river in a small boat on the other side of Corrin Wood. When Murphy and Red Pat arrived, having 'done the job', he took them across the Scalan into Leitrim. Before he left them he gave £8 to Red Pat and £4 to Murphy. Other witnesses corroborated Black Tarry's account, though John Logan, who had been arrested in the first swoop, denied that he had supplied the pistols because he had never owned any firearms, a statement that his daughters later confirmed. The defence lawyer urged the jury not to place any credence in Black Tarry's account. His was the tainted evidence of an approver and he would show that the miscreant had tried to persuade several people from the district to join with him in claiming the reward of £100 offered by the Lord Lieutenant. The *Dublin Evening Mail* of 15 October had carried the text of the order from the Castle. It was worded by the Under-Secretary, Thomas Larcom, and stated that His Excellency was 'pleased to offer a reward One Hundred Pounds to any person who shall within six months from the date hereof, give such information as shall lead to the arrest of the person or persons who committed the same'. The jury were not convinced and returned a verdict of guilty on James Murphy after only two hours.

The charge against Dunne was that of procuring and inciting Patrick Bannon and James Murphy to the murder. Dunne gave the impression of being ill. He fainted several times during the trial and had to be treated by a doctor. The spectators in the crowded courtroom noticed how ill he looked. In hindsight he makes an unlikely candidate for conspiracy. He was rich by the meagre standards of the time and his frustrated political career was hardly sufficient to have driven him to planning the murder of a landlord, especially a female one. There were sensitivities to be considered in those years. Dunne's plea was 'Not guilty.'

McKeon repeated the same evidence that he had given the

previous day during Murphy's hearing. It does not seem to have been relevant to the charge of conspiracy. Black Tarry, however, detailed the whole affair, further claiming that it had begun the previous August — when faced with the evidence of Charlotte's evictions Dunne had declared that with sufficient money he could find someone who would finally eliminate her. Tarry said that he himself had offered £2 but Dunne said it would not be enough and urged Tarry to find more money from the tenants. One of these was James Curry, who later told the court that he had not wished to be involved but had been threatened by Black Tarry. It is hard to work out just how much truth there was in his statements. Tarry admitted that he had had many conversations with Nicholas Kelly, the resident magistrate, who probably groomed McKeon in how to present the evidence in the most damning way. The jury at the commission, who were not necessarily as impartial as they should have been, found Dunne guilty after a mere hour and a quarter. He received the verdict with a notable stoicism, asking merely that his body be delivered to his family for burial. This was granted since the charge of conspiracy was a lesser charge than that of murder. Murphy, however, since found guilty of murder, would be buried in quicklime in the prison yard. The execution, set for 16 May, was the first in Cavan jail for seventeen years.

Dunne's solicitor did what he could to complain about irregularities in the conduct of the trial, especially regarding a possibly biased jury. A petition signed by the bishop of Kilmore and many of his clergy proved ineffective and the chief law lords insisted that the capital sentences stand. A new scaffold was built outside the prison especially for the hanging. The local priests urged their parishioners to stay away but it was too big an event for the younger people to ignore. There was also a certain amount of sectarian approval in the execution of unruly Romanists. The two men received communion in the prison and attended mass twice during the morning of 16 May. Then, at 1pm, Murphy, dressed in white and wearing white gloves, was led out to the platform. According to the *Belfast News Letter* of 19 May, 'at a quarter to twelve the persons in front of the jail numbered about 700 or 800'. Murphy was known to be in the final stages of consumption and his medical condition might have allowed him to cheat the hangman if the appeals procedure had been prolonged. There was a 'loud outburst of horror' when the executioner placed the noose round his neck. He stepped quietly to the trapdoor 'and in a moment was launched into eternity'. His body hung for forty-five minutes until it was cut down by three convicts from the prison.

Dunne was brought from his cell about twenty-five minutes later and stood motionless on the trap. He wore a brown tunic with white cap and gloves and made no comment as the hangman slipped the rope over his head. He dangled for forty minutes before his body was conveyed to his friends. The reporter from the *Freeman's Journal* noted that the body was removed in a cart, 'no hearse being procurable' — a nice way of saying that no Cavan undertaker would handle the funeral. Strangely, most of the crowd left after Murphy's execution and the audience then consisted mainly of a troop of the Eighth Hussars with their officer Captain McNaghten, the Monaghan Militia under Lieut-Colonel Forster, and nearly two hundred police officers. There was no trouble.

Renewed efforts were made to apprehend the elusive Red Pat Bannon, the other presumed murderer. There were several sightings but all proved to be dead ends. The years passed and the thorny Irish Question, which was nearly all about land, rent and impossible landlords began to yield to common sense, aided by the land agitation mentioned earlier and Gladstone's honourable attempt to find a solution. By the end of the nineteenth century people could look back with something like equanimity on the bad old days. Charlotte's murder had all but been forgotten. Then Red Pat returned. He was spotted in Shercock, a town in east Cavan, on the border with Monaghan, in the spring of 1898, more than forty years after the murder. One can only surmise what urge drove him back essentially to face his accusers: homesickness, conscience, drunken bravado? He made no secret of his identity, announcing, it was reported, to fellow drinkers that he was Red Pat Bannon and making a slurred remark, 'I am the shot.'

He was duly taken into custody in Shercock and was charged with the murder of Charlotte Hinds at the larger town of Bailieborough. When he sobered up he retracted his claim to fame; he denied ever having heard of Tubberlion, let alone having ever been there. However Constable Gorby RIC had spent many months tracking him in Ireland and the UK in the years after the murder and, though retired, was able to identify him. In spite of this Red Pat's luck held. After much legal wrangling, the prosecution withdrew from the case, leaving the magistrate with no option but to discharge the prisoner. An outlaw for forty-three years, Red Pat was allowed to walk free. He returned to Liverpool, his home for most of that period.

The killing of Charlotte Hinds was horrible and absolutely inexcusable but little attempt was made to discover the motivation behind such a deed. The British and Unionist press were stern in their blanket condemnation but local papers like the *Anglo-Celt* tried to mitigate their disapproval. What could have driven a prosperous man like Thomas Dunne, who eschewed violence, to conspire against a landlord collecting rents that were her legal due? Such uncharacteristic behaviour was surely evidence of some deep malaise in society. What we can gather of Murphy's character from the newspapers of the time suggests that he does not fit the bill of a cold-blooded killer — he was terminally ill with tuberculosis and had a wife and four children to support.

And what of Charlotte Hinds? Andrew Reilly, the lame man to whom she had given a lift, said during Murphy's trial that she 'was the best-natured woman in the world'. She was certainly a woman with a grievance, almost an avenger of those who had treated her father so badly and hastened his death. She stood at the convergence of two different cultures, one that affirmed the legal rights of landlords to manage their property as they saw fit within the law, the other of a subject people with old dreams of nobility constrained by fate and history to pay rent to a stranger. She could not understand that survival was their main priority and was unaware of how eviction might drive men, seeing wives and children without shelter, to desperate acts. There are Red Pats and the Black Tarrys in all societies, responding in different ways to injustice and expediency. The climate of opinion by the time of Red Pat's hearing had changed over the four decades and wisdom at last prevailed.

3
JAMES MURRAY

ROBERT LLOYD PRAEGAR, the Holywood engineer who preferred being a geologist and primarily botanist, once wrote about Donegal, 'In times so remote that scarcely any portion of the present Ireland was in existence, the rocks of this area were crumpled together and thrown into ridges and hollows running northeast and southwest.' This is almost true of the hollow, between the Derryveagh and Glendowan mountains, that lies west of Letterkenny and contains Lough Veagh, claimed by some to rival Killarney in beauty. It is one of the showpieces of the Glenveagh National Park, which after 150 years of fairly tumultuous history is now one of Ireland's finest amenities. The region was bought by John George Adair in 1857, a man of Scottish descent who hailed from Laois (then Queen's County). He once stood for parliament as an advocate of tenants rights — rather ironic when we consider that as a Donegal landlord his reputation is second only in infamy to that of the third Lord Leitrim.

His estate, which included the territories of Glenveagh, Derryveagh and Gartan, totalled 25,000 acres and he said he acquired it because he was 'enchanted by the surpassing beauty of the scenery'. The statement rings hollow from a man who was reputed to be a hard-dealing land speculator. On the very edge of the lake, on the south bank, he built a castle between 1865 and 1870. Its most notable feature was a keep tower of four storeys with a parapet decorated with battlements. From the beginning Adair was at odds with his tenants; to put it mildly he and they had different perceptions of rights and duties. He enclosed common land and his wild-bird shooting parties moved recklessly through the estate, thus trespassing as far as the tenants were concerned. One day angry tenants interrupted a shoot by surrounding Adair and his friends. He warned them that they would pay for the upset. His habit of impounding stray beasts and charging for their release netted him £395 in the space of a few years. He did everything he could to alienate his smallholders, regarding them as unprofitable nuisances. Their rents were not a great source of income; Cheviot sheep would be far more profitable and he had a precedent in the highland clearances in Scotland when the peasants were evicted to make room for these profitable animals. He decided to become the Irish equivalent of a Scottish laird and felt that an empty glen was desirable.

He began to import sheep from the time of his first acquisition of the land and the shepherds who came to tend his new flocks were rough, violent men who made no attempt to ingratiate themselves with the people of the area. His steward, James Murray, was typical of the agressive Scots who came with the sheep. He claimed in Adair's name compensation for malicious slaughter of sheep but when the police came to investigate the crime they found instead sixty-five animals that had died from exposure and neglect, along with sixteen sheepskins drying in Murray's shed. On Tuesday, 13 November 1860, Murray went to search for missing sheep on the steep slopes above Lough Veagh. Two days later his body was found. His skull had been crushed by a large stone that lay close by, clearly the murder weapon since it had blood and hair on it. It appeared that Murray was just another victim of the informal anti-landlord unrest of the period. Between the time of the acquisition of the estate and the death of Lord Leitrim in 1878 more than a hundred violent deaths had taken place in Ireland.

Adair conveniently assumed that some of his tenants were the assailants which gave him the excuse he needed to clear the glen. It did not matter to him that exhaustive and exhausting enquiries by the police produced no evidence or even suspicion that the Derryveagh tenants were to blame. He evoked the magic word 'Ribbonism', always calculated to ease the consciences of the authorities and their executive arm, the IC. He promptly served eviction notices on all his tenants and because of the perceived threat to public order he was considered to be within his rights. The Church of Ireland rector of Gartan and the local parish priest begged him in vain not to proceed. On 8 April 1861 the most thorough and complete eviction in Ireland since the time of Cromwell took place. Two hundred policemen with a gang of Adair's workers carrying wrecking tools advanced from the southwest at the point where Glenveagh meets Glendowan and cleared the valley. As Jonathan Bardon writes in *A History of Ulster*, it 'took three days to evict 244 people from 46 households and to unroof or level 28 homes over an area of 11,602 acres'. Eventually most of the displaced people were sheltered in the workhouse in Letterkenny, after terrible sufferings and despair. At least one poor man died and another went mad.

The evictions became known internationally and there were three debates in parliament, shaming Sir Robert Peel, Chief Secretary (son of the man who brought us the 'Peelers'), who admitted to having received no official notification about them. Some of the dispossessed were taken out to Australia under a relief scheme organised by Michael O'Grady; some few (about a fifth of the total population) were allowed to return under new leases but most emigrated to the US, settling mainly in the city of Baltimore, the capital of the state of Maryland. Adair completed his fairytale castle in 1870 and died in St Louis, Missouri, in 1885. His American widow, Mrs Cornelia Ritchie, imported Scottish red deer and made the sad and lonely glen one of the finest deerparks in Ireland. The estate was bought in 1937 by a rich American called Henry McIlhenny, who was an actual descendant of one of those evicted. It was he who was responsible for the botanical splendours, especially the Italian garden below the keep with its statues of Ceres and Bacchus. In

1983 McIlhenny donated the demesne and the castle to the Irish people and an interpretative centre was built in 1984 — it is now a popular tourist attraction.

But who killed James Murray? The police investigation centred on a local tenant called Manus Rodden who had been cutting sallies for thatching near the scene and had left a pile near where the body had been found. There was nothing to connect him to the murder apart from that one circumstance. Other locals were questioned but they were not anxious to respond to inquiries from the police, excepting the informant, William Deery, who wished to obtain the reward. He claimed to be a Ribbonman and could name fellow members of the secret society who had killed Murray. As ever, the word Ribbonism was music to the authorities' ears, especially those of the higher ranks of the police force — the ordinary rank and file of the detective branch were not so gullible. Deery said that he saw no less than 120 of Adair's tenants attack and kill the steward. Murray had only time to fire one shot before being overwhelmed. The bullet, Deery claimed, had wounded a tenant called Bradley. An examination by detectives of the scene showed that there were no footprints or disturbance of the surrounding vegetation, nothing to suggest that a mob had gathered there. There was no trace of anybody called Bradley in the glen and the only arrest made in the Murray case was that of Deery who got seven years for perjury.

If this were a fictional story made for television old telly hands would have thought Adair himself as the most likely culprit. The murder played into his hands, presenting him with the perfect excuse to clear the glen, which gives him a motive. However, the more likely story, never proven by the police, was that Murray's wife had him killed, conniving with her lover, Dugald Rankin, the Murrays' lodger. A Donegal magistrate, Theobald Dillon RM, wrote to Sir Thomas Larcom, the permanent Under-Secretary, to say that he believed this rumour and that the actual perpetrator was Archibald Campbell, another of the rough Scottish shepherds, who was simply carrying out Rankin's orders. Rankin and Mrs Murray were seen embracing in her kitchen by Adam Grierson, another shepherd. It was believed that Rankin had interfered with the gun that Murray carried, fixing it so that it could only fire one shot and that it would jam if the trigger were pulled again. The police also believed in this conspiracy theory. JF Maguire, the member for Donegal, in one of several debates about the Adair evictions, stated that there was a man in Donegal who was openly suspected of the crime. It could not be proved that he was the culprit but it was noted at Murray's funeral that he wore the dead man's suit and was 'extremely intimate' with the dead man's wife.

The shepherds from Scotland continued to behave in a near criminal fashion. Rankin shot and wounded an IC man in the hand during an ale-house brawl in Strabane in March 1861, four months after Murray's death. He was sent to jail for two years. Grierson, who was promoted to Murray's job as steward, was arrested after he shot one tenant and attacked another. He was dismissed from his post in 1862 for embezzling Adair's money. Then, in April 1863, he was mortally wounded in an ambush and tried to incriminate the son of a tenant even while dying. The charges against the tenant were later dropped. Eventually a kind of peace settled on the dark Glenveagh.

Glenveagh today rejoices in its reputation as one of Ireland's premier national parks and the beauty of the glen is undiminished. Sometimes the red deer cross over into Glendowan, startling motorists on the road to Doochary, and as one drives from Doochary to Churchill, it is possible to look down into the once troubled glen and its fjord-like lough. It is hard to picture it now as a place of sadness and danger but it certainly was in April 1861 when, as the *Londonderry Standard* reported, 'the police officers themselves could not refrain from weeping'.

4
WILLIAM GLASS

THE COUNTY TYRONE TOWN OF NEWTOWNSTEWART lies picturesquely around a loop of the River Mourne, which is called the Foyle between Strabane and Derry, and the Strule between the town and Omagh, ten and a quarter miles away. The Derg (flowing from penitential Lough Derg) joins the Mourne about three miles to the northwest, and the Owenkillew, that changes the name of the river, meets it just below the town. The estate of the Duke of Abercorn at Baronscourt with its two hills, Bessie Bell and Mary Gray, dominates Newtownstewart. Like many 'new' towns it had its Gaelic name replaced during the seventeenth century Ulster plantation. In 1628 Sir William Stewart renamed what was once *Lioslas* (perhaps 'place of the fort') as a memorial to himself. The hills, which also had ancient Gaelic names, were christened by an early duke after the tragic heroines of a Lowland ballad collected by Sir Walter Scott. Few inland settlements are set so beautifully near the confluence of three very fishy rivers. It is now mainly a market town and angling centre but it had an industrial past concerned with linen and limestone quarrying.

It was, during the mid-nineteenth century, a significant stop on the main Derry to Dublin permanent way as part of the Londonderry and Enniskillen Railway, later the Great Northern Railway, and described by the *Londonderry Sentinel* on 4 July 1871 as a 'thriving prosperous town'. Its branch of the Northern Banking Company was quite busy, having a sub-office in the village of Drumquin, ten miles away. On Thursday, 29 June 1871, it was manned by the teller, William Glass, from Templepatrick in County Antrim, the manager, JG Strahan, having travelled to Drumquin to preside at the bank's office which opened on market and fair days. Glass, though perfectly happy as a bank teller, preferred the more adventurous prospect of life in the RIC. He had befriended the new local head of the RIC, Sub-Inspector Thomas Montgomery, who had been transferred to the town in March from Newtownards, and lived in McClenaghan's hotel with his wife. Montgomery had originally been a clerk with the Belfast Bank and was in an ideal position to advise Glass about the route that he himself had taken.

The bank, as was customary until very recently, was also the home of the manager. Strahan's wife and family were off on holiday but his unmarried aunt, Mary Thompson, was staying with him as relief housekeeper. She was in the upstairs parlour at 2.30pm when Inspector Montgomery climbed the stairs to ask about Strahan. She was not long back from seeing Montgomery's wife whom she had visited about 1pm. The subinspector had been there when she called and offered her a glass of wine, which she refused. The domestic staff in the bank house consisted of a maid, Fanny McBride, and Robert Cook, a lad who worked in the garden. It was he who opened the door separating the residential part of the building from the official bank premises when Miss Thompson knocked on her return from her visit. Montgomery's purpose with Strahan was to see if he was free to go fishing that evening and he was told that the manager (a keen angler) would not be back until 5pm.

At about 4pm Fanny left her kitchen to check the time by the bank clock that could be seen through the glass door. To her horror Glass was lying on the floor covered in blood. She ran to her temporary mistress who told her to fetch James McDowall, the owner of the hardware store across the street. As the *Londonderry Sentinel* reported on Tuesday 4 July, she told him the 'something terrible had happened to Mr Glass'. McDowall pushed open the bank door and, when he saw the condition of the young bank clerk, immediately sent for Sub-Inspector

Montgomery who, as the senior police officer in the town, should be the first to be informed, and for Dr John Todd MD. The latter did not arrive until 6.30pm and his examination revealed that the deceased's head had no fewer than ten wounds, any of which could have been mortal, and that a file with a brass base had been driven through one ear into the brain. As the *Sentinel* detailed:

> It would appear from the surrounding circumstances that the deceased was approaching the fire-proof safe in the inner office when he received the first blow... A map suspended on a wall near the safe is greatly bespattered with blood, and a door leading to the outer office of the bank had blood and hair sticking to it. This same door has several other marks indicative of a fearful struggle. One part is slightly splintered, as if by a chopper or cleaver, and the surface has several dents or marks, apparently caused by a blunt instrument. Immediately opposite the door which opens inward to the private office, there is a hole in the lath-and-plaster into which a file, exactly similar to that of the deceased, fits. Near this spot was found a handful of black hair unlike that of the deceased whose hair was brown and curly.

The reporter from the *Londonderry Journal* filed copy dated Friday night, which appeared in the paper on Saturday 1 July. He had been allowed to view the body, 'a very horrifying spectacle'. He also reported that 'the face bore no trace of agony. The expression was rather of surprise, with a touch of determination.' He noted that the deceased 'was a young, athletic man, several years on this side of thirty'. He had come from the head office in Belfast some years previously, 'remained for some time in Derry and was thence transferred to Newtownstewart'. By the time the *Sentinel* appeared on the Tuesday it was known and reported by the paper that County Inspector Heard and Sub-Inspectors Hogben and Hunter had charge of the case, and that the Northern Banking Company was offering a reward of £100 for information leading to the conviction of the murderer and £60 for private information. Boxes containing silver and gold had not been touched but £1,520 in notes had been taken.

These constabulary officers were, however, not the first on the scene. Montgomery arrived at 5pm, about twenty minutes after the local magistrate, Commander Scott. They examined the room and Scott was startled by Montgomery's suggestion that Glass might have committed suicide. It was an extremely odd thing for a high-ranking, experienced police officer to say about a body with severe head wounds and a metal spike through its ear. Scott was also dismayed that Montgomery intended to disturb the crime scene by having Glass's body removed.

The following day an inquest was set up in an assembly room built by Samuel Hood in Main Street. McDowall, from the hardware store, stated that he had seen Montgomery come out of the bank at about 3.30pm: 'He had what appeared to be a waterproof coat on his arm. He went to the back street.' A whole hour and a half elapsed before the Sub-Inspector's return to the bank and his preposterous suggestion about the cause of death.

Head Constable Hobson, Montgomery's second-in-command, had spent the day of the murder in Drumquin. It was the fair day in the village and it was customary to supplement the usual police presence with an experienced and high-ranking officer. It proved to be a wearisome day with the usual amount of trouble associated with drink. He was glad to stop in for a glass himself when he returned to Newtownstewart that evening. When he heard about the murder he went at once to the scene and made a complete search of the two rooms that constituted the bank premises. Hobson was thorough and intensely ambitious, and he was horrified to learn that Montgomery had not followed correct protocol. He should have informed each of the five nearest police stations as well as Derry, Omagh and Dublin about the murder. He agreed with Scott that 'death in suspicious circumstances' was an inadequate description. Hobson was likewise concerned that the lack of proper procedure would redound badly on the Newtownstewart barracks as a whole. He would have to share in any official criticism of Montgomery's actions — or lack of them. Montgomery, sensing his junior colleague's irritation, urged him to go to his lodgings and get some rest. Hobson made the same suggestion to his superior with some asperity and more reason, since Montgomery was showing signs of strain and acting peculiarly.

However, the Sub-Inspector did not return to his hotel (and was afterwards chided by the proprietor's daughter who had sat up all night to let him in). He headed out instead on the Omagh Road towards a local spot called Grangewood, which he had visited that afternoon. On his way he was met by a horse car with several RIC constables and Inspector William F Purcell from Omagh. Purcell hailed his colleague and joined him to walk back to Newtownstewart. Montgomery furnished Purcell with all details of the fatality and both expressed their shock that such a thing could happen in a respectable town. The two men arrived at the bank house and went inside. While Purcell was examining the scene he noticed that two pieces of carpet were missing and wondered if they had been bloodstained and whether they had been sent for forensic examination. Montgomery said he did not know but he then asked Purcell for his professional opinion as to whether the last person seen leaving the bank could be convicted of murder 'if he had no blood on his clothes'. Purcell dismissed the suggestion immediately saying that circumstantial evidence was almost impossible as a basis for conviction. Then Montgomery admitted that he had visited the bank house around the likely time of the murder. The startled Purcell said nothing, perhaps thinking that Montgomery had been very affected by the murder. The two policemen walked back out the Omagh Road until Purcell was picked up again by his horse car.

The inquest took four weeks with the witnesses being questioned closely about visitors to the bank, and which doors were open or shut — whether the servant girl, Fanny McBride, had left the door ajar when she had been dealing with the 'cockle men'. These were regular visitors in season to the town, which lay on their commercial route from Lettermacaward on the Gweebarra River estuary in West Donegal. Hugh Bonnar and Mickey Gallagher were afterwards called as witnesses but had nothing helpful to contribute; Bonnar used the bank stop to feed his mare with a bag of oats and, though Gallagher had been conscious of someone leaving the bank, he could not attempt a description. As the inquest continued on its tedious way it became clear that Montgomery was a significant witness. He had been seen putting his head out of the main bank door, looking up and down the street, and then withdrawing again. Shortly afterwards he was seen leaving the building and heading to the back street. Asked by the coroner, William Orr, as to why he had checked the street before leaving he said he had gone back for his stick. Montgomery was advised to seek legal representation; as Sub-Inspector Hogben remarked, 'There is allegation by inference.'

The inquest had been adjourned on the Saturday, the day of Glass's funeral. As the reporter from the *Londonderry Journal* reported on Monday, 3 July:

> On Saturday the remains of Mr Glass were removed from Mr Kerr's hotel, Newtownstewart, to the railway station for conveyance by train via Omagh and Portadown, to Templepatrick, county Antrim, of which place deceased was a native. Although at the time rain fell in torrents, a larger assemblage, not only of the inhabitants of the town, but also of the surrounding district, testified their respect for the lamented deceased by following his remains, which were conveyed in a hearse, to the railway station.

The *Journal* piece concluded with the ominous words, 'Sub-

Inspector Montgomery is still guarded in his room.' The *Belfast News Letter* sent its own reporter who headed his account in the edition of Saturday, 1 July: 'Horrible Murder and Robbery' and slightly improperly anticipated the inquest's findings with Monday's headline: 'Arrest of Sub-Inspector Montgomery'.

After four weeks of argument, many witnesses and lots of repetitive evidence, there was little else the jury could do but find Montgomery guilty of the murder of his friend Glass. Their verdict was that Montgomery 'with malice aforethought murdered William Glass on Thursday 29 June 1871'. He was removed from the Newtownstewart barracks in handcuffs and placed in prison in Omagh until his trial. It is a principle of murder detection that one looks for motive, opportunity, the murder weapon and convincing forensics. Montgomery certainly had opportunity but by the putative date for the trial the weapon had not been discovered. There also lacked an apparent motive and not one of the witnesses who saw Montgomery leave the bank that day had noticed any blood on his clothing. The trial had to be postponed. The missing £1,520 in notes had been unearthed not long after the killing in Grangewood. Then, before the New Year, a kind of breakthrough occurred: the murder weapon was found in Grangewood, not far from where the money had been discovered. It was a billhook, an agricultural tool used for taming unruly hedges. It has a curved blade, as the name implies, and a long handle to enable the farmer (or gardener) to reach the higher hedges. This one still had blood and hairs on it and it was found that the handle had been weighted with lead shot to make the implement more vicious. Glass's body was exhumed and Dr Todd, who had pronounced at the scene in June, confirmed that it was a weapon capable of making the gashes in the deceased's head.

The technique of fingerprint identification, though centuries old, was only refined as a science at the very end of the nineteenth century by Sir Francis Galton and not adopted for

British police use until 1901. The investigators could not prove that Montgomery had handled the billhook using fingerprints, and the witnesses who had seen him leave the bank saw no trace of either blood or billhook. The detectives, however, had discovered a motive when they investigated Montgomery's financial situation. It transpired that he was in serious financial difficulties. He had lost a lot of money in stock market speculation — his own, his father-in-law's, and even cash invested with him by junior members of the force at his own barracks. (He had been careful to pay supposed dividends to the constables to persuade them of the wisdom of their investments.)

The case finally came to court, after several postponements, in July 1872. The presiding Judge Lawson refused to allow the prosecution to reveal that Montgomery had a very powerful motive with his financial troubles. Without this important information all evidence was circumstantial and, despite effective pleading by the prosecution team, the jury could not agree. Lawson sent them back for further deliberation for a further five hours but they failed once again to reach a unanimous verdict. The judge had no alternative but to thank them for their attention and dismiss them. Montgomery's trial was put off to the next assizes.

The second trial opened the following March but this time there was a marked difference. The courtroom was still crowded with spectators and it was with some satisfaction that they heard the prosecution disclose the very cogent motive of Montgomery's financial straits. Judge Barry, who presided at this second trial, gave permission for that crucial information to be revealed to the jury. The main defence counsel spoke for ten hours, exhausting himself in the process. He concentrated upon what was assumed about Montgomery's character — his honourable record and the ultra-respectability of his background. He also repeated that there was nothing furtive about Montgomery's leaving the bank on that June afternoon.

WILLIAM GLASS

There was absolutely no indication that he was carrying the billhook or more than £1,500 in notes. His clothes were free of bloodstains and there was no sign of the weapon. His arguments persuaded at least two members of the jury and Barry had to accept that there would be no agreement in this trial. He postponed it again, fixing a new date for 21 July 1873, more than two years after Glass's death.

Montgomery's third and final trial was presided over once again by Judge Barry. It lasted seven days. The public galleries were crowded with sightseers, and local papers were full of it, recording every minute detail. A significant part of the evidence was concerned with the lack of bloodstains on Montgomery's clothes, the disposal of the money and the concealment of the weapon. The apparent lack of motive had been dispelled when Judge Barry in the second trial permitted the prosecution to reveal that the accused was deeply in debt. This was damning but Montgomery lost all credence when the Crown had a constable about the same build as the accused stand on a table in the middle of the court, wearing the clothes that Montgomery wore on the day of the killing. There was no trace of blood — in his cell he told reporters that he had sponged off any 'sparks' before he left the bank premises — and the constable was responsible for quite a few gasps in the courtroom when he produced notes amounting to at least £1,500 from different pockets. Even more dramatic was the officer's statement that he had the handle of the billhook in a trouser pocket and the fearsome blade wrapped in newspaper between shirt and waistcoat. With modern forensic techniques Montgomery's guilt would have been discovered by the second day (the pieces of hair that were manifestly not Glass's and DNA would have fixed him from the start) but then with modern legal practice he would not have been hanged and perhaps found to have sufficient mental imbalance to have been detained at the Queen's pleasure in a secure mental hospital. It was clear that, in spite of the efforts of the defence team, he was seen to be guilty beyond a reasonable doubt. The juries in all three trials had been notable for interaction with counsel and even the judges, asking questions directly and showing an indecorous lack of proper demeanour in court. At last they seemed to be satisfied. They had sat for seven days and, on the seventh, listened for seven hours that Monday, 28 July, as Judge Barry 'charged' the jury.

It was a long speech and, since judges were regarded with great awe and reverence, listened to with great attention and not just by the jury. It was slightly condescending but elaborate in its summary of the case, and fulsome in its praise of both legal teams: 'The case has been conducted both on behalf of the Crown and the prisoner with the most consummate ability.' So detailed was the judge's summary that it required a great deal of concentration to follow the twists and turns of the story. They persevered and when told to retire to find a verdict did so in less than half an hour. Fatigue may have played its part in the speed of their achieving unanimity but it was now clear that Montgomery had motive, opportunity and murder weapon, and could, as the constable demonstrated, have smuggled the billhook and money under clothes that showed no signs of blood or hair.

Found guilty, Montgomery responded to the judge's question, 'Have you anything to say why sentence should not be passed upon you?' with a speech as bizarre as it was unconvincing. After thanking the judge for his impartiality he startled the court by claiming that around the time of the murder he was not in his right mind:

> In the month of June 1870 I was invited to Mile Cross, the residence of Mr Bradshaw [his future wife's clergyman uncle], and at that time I was in the enjoyment of good health. I was there delusively drugged and poisoned for the purpose of rendering me weak-minded. When I went to the doctor he told me I had only a few days to live... In that state I consented to marry... In the month of

WILLIAM GLASS

> November I embarked on this foolish, ridiculous speculation, during which I lost large sums of money, much larger than have appeared in evidence... I then became ambitious and the monomania of attacking banks took possession of me. I told my own orderly on one occasion when I was going to Holywood that I would go to the bank, kill the cashier, take the money with me to Cave Hill, and there build a house. When I came to Newtownstewart I was in a state of complete derangement... I never intended and would not have not injured any man had I not been demented...

He continued in this vein for some time and, though Judge Barry was visibly affected, he proceeded with sentencing. He drew attention to the heinousness of the crime before God and man, speaking at the same length as Montgomery. Finally he had 'to pass the dreadful sentence of the law' and putting on the black cap uttered the chilling formula:

> The sentence and judgment of the Court is, and I do adjudge it, that you, Thomas Hartley Montgomery, be taken from the bar of this court at which you now stand to the place from whence you came, in the common gaol of county Tyrone; and that you be taken on Tuesday, the 26th day of August, in the year of our Lord, 1873, to the common place of execution within the prison in which you are then found, and then and there hanged by the neck until you are dead; and that your body be buried within the precincts of the prison. And may the Lord have mercy on your soul.

There was no reprieve or any response to his plea of insanity, though the MacNaghten rules had been formulated in 1843. Montgomery was hanged in Omagh Jail on the day specified by Judge Barry. The reporter of the *Londonderry Standard*, which was printed the day after the event, made the most of nearly two full columns of two inches width, set in tiny 8-point. From the start he was pointed about the malefactor's loss of status. In earlier accounts of the various trials he had referred to him as Sub-Inspector Thomas Hartley Montgomery. Now his headline read 'Execution of the Convict Montgomery'. The deed was done 'at precisely eight o'clock' as one of 'the most private of any private execution which has yet taken place in the kingdom'. The reporter blamed 'the arbitrary and unwarrantable conduct of the Board of Governors of the Gaol, represented by the Sub-Sheriff, in excluding the representatives of the Press'. His editor made the exclusion the subject of a bitter editorial in the next number of the paper. The anonymous reporter admitted that 'an execution under such circumstances was perhaps a fitting *denouement* to the dreadful tragedy of which it was the closing scene'.

The 'unhappy culprit' was reported as being 'deadly pale' and 'wearing the same dress (black frock-coat and vest, and light coloured trousers, with dark stripes) which he wore during the three successive trials'. The flowing black and silver beard did not after all have to be shaved off as was expected, thanks to the skill of the hangman who was, as reported, an Englishman, who appeared to be 'about fifty or fifty-five years of age'. The hangman became the centre of morbid attention in Omagh station as he sat waiting waiting for the Derry train. He was clearly 'not a man of weak nerve' as he sat smoking a cigar and 'formed the centre of attraction for the large crowd assembled on the platform'. Of many gruesome details given about the actual process of execution one sentence will suffice: 'There was no violent struggling, a slight quivering of the right foot being the only visible sign of expiring life.'

The case remains fascinating; the idea of the primary detective being the killer is ingenious, and has been used by Agatha Christie and others. It was terribly shocking at the time. The RIC was highly respected with a reputation for honesty and respectability, unlike the often venal local constabularies that they replaced. To think that a respected authority figure should prove villain was hard for the sober citizens of County Tyrone to stomach. It was typical of ingrained attitudes that the *Londonderry Sentinel* commented in its first report, on Tuesday, 4 July 1871, long before Montgomery was widely suspected, that this kind of crime might be characteristic of Connacht or Munster but not of ultra-respectable Ulster:

> We in the North are unused to such things. Had such a case happened in the South or West we would be inclined to pronounce it awful or deplorable; but occurring in our midst we are disposed to think it incredible.

Interesting, too, was the mindset of the killer. Did he really think that his bumbling over the cause of death, his naïve speculation in conversation with Willie Purcell from Omagh as to whether a lack of bloodstains on clothes would exonerate a killer, and his unexplained absence between 3.30 and 5pm on the day of the murder, would not convince people of his having questions to answer?

His claim of insanity at the end of the third trial was dismissed and yet some kind of madness drove him to kill his friend and pupil — he was coaching Glass for entrance to the RIC. Undoubtedly, he was desperate for cash because of his unsuccessful speculations on the Stock Exchange. Any suggestion of financial irregularity, especially peculation of his subordinates' money after fake promises of investment, would have meant the end of his promising career in the service. His plan was clearly not to filch the cash when Glass's attention was distracted but rather to engage in armed robbery. His careful preparation of the chief murder weapon, the billhook with the weighted handle, suggested a cool determination to do violence. He had bought lead from McDowall, ostensibly to make bullets for a musketry course he was attending. He told McDowall later that he had lost most of the lead in the fire but nineteen ounces had been found in the handle of the billhook. His demeanour after the discovery of Glass's body was that of a man extremely agitated and his second-in-command, Head Constable Hobson, was shocked that Montgomery had not informed the five RIC out-stations of the event.

There is a marked contrast between the calculated planning of the murder and the fraying of his resolve afterwards. Perhaps he was appalled by what he had done; when the full realisation of the cruelty of the *modus operandi* sank in he may have been as horrified as his colleagues and neighbours. The driving of the file spike into Glass's ear after death was inexplicably cruel. The case remains fascinating because of the character of the murderer and his relationship with his young victim. There are many questions one would have liked to ask Montgomery if you could trust the answers of such a fantasist. Questioned on Omagh jail's equivalent of Death Row he claimed that the killing had been accomplished before he went up to Mary Thompson and that even as he established his spurious reason for being in the bank house — asking her what time the manager would return as he wished to go fishing with him — he said there had been 'sparks' of blood on his clothing. (Strahan afterwards looked perplexed since he had never gone fishing with Montgomery nor was aware that the Sub-Inspector had any interest in angling.)

If you mention the Newtownstewart bank murder in Ulster's north-west today they will say: 'That's the one where the murderer was the detective!'

5
THE THIRD EARL OF LEITRIM

OF THAT OFTEN JUSTLY EXECRATED CLASS, the Irish landlord, none received more execration than William Sydney Clements, the third Earl of Leitrim. He was cordially detested by his peasant tenants throughout his many properties, but most especially in the part of Donegal in which he preferred to live, building his favourite Big House, Manorvaughan, not far from Carrigart. His family had a tradition of building. In 1751 one ancestor, Nathaniel Clements, constructed the house in Phoenix Park which became the Vice-Regal Lodge and is now *Áras an Uachtaráin*. The family came over with Cromwell and by the time Nathaniel's son, Robert, had become the first Earl of Leitrim in 1795 he had estates in Leitrim, Galway, Kildare and Donegal. The second Earl, also Nathaniel, was a benevolent landlord, active in alleviating the hardships of the 1822 potato famine and proving in all respects to be a kindly and generous man. His son Robert died of tuberculosis in 1839 and so Robert's younger brother, William, at forty-eight years, acceded to the title on his death in 1854 and to large properties in Leitrim and Donegal.

William had followed the usual career of a younger son who had no interest in being a clergyman; he joined the army and had a successful military career, ending as a lieutenant-colonel. He represented County Leitrim at the Westminster Parliament (1839–47) and after succeeding sat in the House of Lords as Lord Leitrim. He was also a magistrate for Donegal, Galway and Leitrim and colonel of the Leitrim militia. His Donegal tenants had lived in amity with his father and felt they had little to fear from the younger son. As chairman of the Mohill Board of Guardians in 1848 he had done good work in famine relief in Leitrim. He certainly was not that abomination, an absentee landlord, but by the time he had got into his stride most of his tenants heartily wished he was.

He was a tall man and very strong, and from the moment he became the third earl he seemed to have reverted to the stance of a medieval baron who demanded absolute subservience from his serfs. In all his estates, totalling 94,535 acres and with a valuation of £19,692 he assumed utter control of most aspects of life, being particularly exacting in matters of rent and improvement. He disregarded the long-cherished Ulster Custom, ignoring the 'three Fs' of fair rent, fixity of tenure and free sale. His actions suggested that whatever had been the practice in other parts of Ulster there would be no 'three Fs' on his Donegal estates. His penchant for litigation meant that a lot of his income went on lawyers' fees. He prosecuted more than one-fifteenth of his tenants on his 57,000-acre estate, in Donegal. This acreage included land on both sides of Mulroy Bay with the village of Milford as its natural centre. Perhaps inevitably he was finally murdered in his seventy-second year, along with his driver and clerk, on 2 April 1878 at Woodquarter, on the west shore of Mulroy.

The rage he exhibited in all his dealings and the absolute obedience that he expected from those he regarded as his underlings might imply that he was intermittently in the grip of some mania. It was not only his tenants with whom he felt at odds; members of his own class despised and detested him. A long-standing feud with Lord Carlisle, the Lord-Lieutenant of Ireland, caused him to fill the Maam Hotel, which lay within his Galway estate, with his own tenants, knowing that Carlisle intended to stay there on an official tour of Connemara. His views on education, too, were original. He forbade the children in the National Schools on his estates to have books for homework for the following three reasons: (i) the children could not afford to buy them; (ii) they had no time to study at home because they should be helping their parents on the farms; (iii) if they learned at home the teachers would have nothing to do.

More serious was the accusation that he applied the principle of *droit de seigneur* as far as the daughters of his tenants were concerned. This accusation may well be unjust. He was unmarried but clearly fond of women and liked their company. He was not the only landlord to be so accused but the practice of 'tally women' belonged to an earlier age. It is now generally accepted that his perceived licentious life was not the reason for his killing. Leitrim's defenders claimed that if a girl from his estate found herself pregnant by whatever father she received a good deal of sympathy if she claimed that the Earl had forced himself upon her. The charge that he regarded his tenants' daughters as fair game was levelled after his death by members of the Irish Party in the House of Commons, believing the stories that were current in the area and generally held throughout nationalist Ireland. He was more likely to have been targeted because of his refusal to grant 'tenant right' even though the 1870 Landlord and Tenant Act had made the practice legal (and not just at the whim of the landlord). The Earl was not, however, going to regard himself bound by acts of parliament, especially those passed by Gladstone whom he probably regarded as an extreme anarchist.

Another more likely cause of the hatred felt by his tenantry was his practice of apparently arbitrary evictions. These 'legal' proceedings included the sequestration of a Catholic church at Gortletteragh in County Leitrim, using a force of 1,000 soldiers and policemen. They were faced by 6,000 protestors who gathered from Longford, Roscommon and Westmeath, as well as locals. Serious trouble was prevented only by the actions of the parish priest. Then, as if to demonstrate how even-handed he was, the Earl proceeded with equal energy against the Rev Robert White, the Presbyterian minister of Milford. White had made extensive improvements on his property costing £450.

Leitrim immediately raised the rent in blatant contravention of one of the 'three Fs'. When White refused to pay he was evicted.

The 1870s in Ireland were a time of great unrest culminating in the beginning of the Land War in 1879. Secret agrarian societies such as the Ribbonmen had long regarded landlords as legitimate targets during the Tithe Wars of the 1830s and there were still residual elements of these societies in different parts of the country. The Molly Maguires (so called because they dressed in women's dresses on their raids), formed with the specific intention of attacking landlords in the 1840s, were one such. Another name to conjure with was Fenian, popular with the peasantry since the society was founded by James Stephens in 1858.

Leitrim's estates included the Fanad Peninsula where there was a tradition of, at least, non-cooperation, if not active resistance. Leitrim's death resulted from the final successful attempt on his life; there had previous attempts. These may have been perpetrated by a few local people or even individuals, while the weapons could have been supplied by a wider organisation, perhaps a rogue branch of a secret society. Locals tended to associate themselves with one of these organisations, borrowing the name for publicity purposes. The Earl was a hands-on landlord. He conducted regular inspections of all his properties, paying particular attention to his Donegal estates. This risky practice was another example of his almost perverse sense of indestructibility and manic belief in his power over the tenants. The killing took place nearly 130 years ago and the story had since become more and more fanciful with the perpetrators elevated to the status of heroes. In 1960 a memorial cross was erected in Kindrum at the top of the Fanad Peninsula with the inscription:

> Erected to the memory of the three Fanad Patriots, Neil Shiels, Doughmore, Michael Heraghty, Tullyconnell, Michael McElwee, Ballywhoriskey who by their heroism

> in Cratlagh Wood on the morning of April 2nd 1878 ended
> the tyranny of landlordism.

A version in Irish is also carved on the base of the cross.

In general the murder of Lord Leitrim has become part of the *béaloideas* of Irish folklore, with elements of sleight of hand if not actual magic. When Leitrim travelled on inspection tours in Donegal he was usually accompanied by a guard of RIC officers, who went out from Milford to Manorvaughan to accompany him into the town where it was felt he might not be safe. On the morning of his death there was no police escort because his lordship left an hour earlier than was his custom. It is held in local tradition that all the clocks in Manorvaughan had been put forward one hour to make sure that he left without his usual bodyguards. It is also believed that one of his outdoor workers, Dan O'Loughlin, was a Ribbonman and it was he who gave advance notice of Leitrim's movements to the killers.

At first the campaign was rather economic than murderous. It was decided to make life as miserable and dangerous as possible for Leitrim's bailiffs so that they could no longer work for him. By this means they hoped to ruin him because without land agents the estates could not be run properly. Leitrim would have to concentrate all his energies on estate management and would not be able to be omnipresent. However, as fast as they frightened one bailiff off there was always another willing to take his place.

According to Liam Dolan, who wrote a fascinating account of the event in *The Third Earl of Leitrim*, it was Leitrim's treatment of his tenant, Mandy Callaghan, who allowed a school to be built on his holding at Coolderry (on the north coast west of Fanad Head) without the permission of his landlord that finally hardened attitudes. He began the process of eviction and the case went against Callaghan at Lifford Assizes on 28 March 1878. Callaghan is believed to have been the leader of the local Fenians (whatever that title may actually have implied) and it was he who sanctioned the extreme remedy. Leitrim was killed five days later.

An earlier attempt to kill the Earl had failed when Leitrim cancelled an inspection of the Fanad properties of his estate. On another occasion it was discovered that his lordship used to, when the weather was fine, walk with a lady friend on a path by a limekiln about a mile from Manorvaughan. Three men rowed to the west shore of Mulroy Bay and lay concealed near the kiln for about thirty-six hours. Leitrim came strolling down the path with his friend and it seemed that nothing could save him when one of the assailants fainted from fatigue and tension. After Mandy Callaghan's court case failed, a much more elaborate plan that had been hatching since the winter of 1877, was given the go-ahead. Members of two secret societies joined forces in the spring of 1878. The men chosen were those commemorated on the Kindrum Cross, Michael McElwee, Neil Sheils and Michael Heraghty. McElwee was known in his home place of Ballywhoriskey as *'Mickey Rua'* because of his long red hair and beard. He was a Ribbonman and enormously strong. Sheils, a journeyman tailor, was called *'An Tailliúir Rua'* because he shared the same colouring as McElwee. He had an eviction served upon him that would leave his wife and four children homeless and destitute. Heraghty was also a tailor and an active Fenian and had a local reputation as a marksman. He was to prepare the guns.

On 29 March Leitrim travelled from Derry on the horse omnibus belonging to Jury's Hotel. He was accompanied as usual by his valet, William Kincaid, and his clerk, John Makim. They took the ferry from Fahan to the east shore, having arranged for a driver to meet the party at 1pm on the following Tuesday, 2 April. Leitrim intended to travel to his County Leitrim estates to supervise evictions near Lough Rynn. That day was chosen for the attack. Heraghty got his hands on a muzzle-loader and a new stock that he had had made locally; Callaghan provided another muzzle-loader. There were also

THE THIRD EARL OF LEITRIM

three muzzle-loading pistols. The three rowed five miles across Mulroy Bay, reaching Woodquarter around 7am on Tuesday morning. They hid in the Cratlagh Wood mentioned on the Kindrum Cross, which Leitrim himself had planted. The car carrying Leitrim went at a good lick on the road to Milford. The spot chosen was where the road had a sudden dip and Charles Buchanan, the driver, had to slow down. He was the first victim of the attack, blown out of the dickey by the ball that killed him. Makim the clerk was next to fall; he died some time later.

Leitrim's left shoulder was shattered and he seems to have been unable to return fire from his pistol. He was seventy-two years old but such was his temperament that he turned to confront his attackers. McElwee and Sheils fired again and shattered the landlord's arm. There was no time to reload so Mickey *Rua* hurled himself at Leitrim who caught him by the beard with his good right arm and pulled him nearly to the ground. Sheils came up behind him and, using his empty gun, hit Leitrim on the skull with the stock. The blow killed Leitrim instantly though he remained gripped to McElwee's beard. Sheils had to cut him free. They dragged the Earl's body to a pool of water by the side of the road and left the dead man lying face down. The gunstock lay in pieces at the scene but McElwee and Sheils had either forgotten about it or were more anxious to escape, rowing as hard as they could to the eastern shore of the bay. It is part of the folklore that every man in Fanad with a red beard shaved it off to protect McElwee, who presumably shaved his off too. Perhaps because he had some foreknowledge that something could happen, Michael Logue, the driver of the other car, may have arranged for his horse to go lame. He and William Kincaid, Leitrim's valet, were too far behind to be in danger. The two men arrived to find Buchanan's body and have poor Makim, who had been shot behind the ear, stagger towards them. Kincaid jumped down from Logue's car and rendered what help he could to the clerk. He had witnessed the final moments of Leitrim's life, hearing the crack as the red stock of

Heraghty's gun brained his master.

Kincaid moved Buchanan's body to the side of the narrow road so that Logue could bring up his car. They gently propped Makim against the ditch and found Leitrim's body face down in the pool of water. Buchanan's empty car had been pulled up the road in the opposite direction by the frightened horse — a local boy had given chase, climbed up into the driver's seat and managed to pull it to a halt. Kincaid relieved the boy of his charge and turned the car towards Milford again. It did not take him long to cover a distance of about three miles. He shouted his ghastly news to all he met on the journey, including the two policemen who were on their way to act as guards for His Lordship. Constable James Rourke, an RIC officer from Kerrykeel barracks, on the east bank of Mulroy, discovered the remains of Heraghty's gun with its painted red stock. It lay under the stern seat of the boat which took McElwee and Sheils to the Fanad side of the bay. They were lucky not to be apprehended by the same policeman who had passed their landfall on his way to Milford that morning.

Heraghty, who had been chosen because of his expertise with firearms, had inexplicably been sent as lookout and played little part in the attack. He established a kind of alibi by making his way to holy Doon Well, a local shrine. He arrived at a house where he was known, four miles away on the road to Kilmacrenan, telling the *bean á tí* that he had been to Doon Well for water for his mother whose sight was failing. Sheils went to the house where he was working as a tailor, as if for a normal day's work, and McElwee arrived at his home in Ballyhooriskey on the north coast and fell to his trade of making lobster pots out of willow sallies. The job had been done and now they had to await the consequences.

The bodies were found by two local men, John Clarke and John McBride. They lifted Leitrim's body out of the pool where McElwee and Sheils had dumped it. Buchanan's body lay where Kincaid had placed it and Makim was still propped against the ditch on the Manorvaughan road. He was barely alive and unable to speak; he died a short while later on the way to Milford. A gun, pistol and the remains of Heraghty's stock were collected and handed to Constable Maguire, who had arrived from Milford. The investigation was led by County Inspector Peter Carr who came from his headquarters in Letterkenny as soon as he heard about the shooting — proving the wire telegraph to be quite efficient for its time. A search of the place showed two flattened patches where McElwee and Sheils had laid waiting in ambush. Constable Doudican, Carr's assistant, found a pistol between the two patches. They also found a hat and a bottle with a broken neck which smelt of the poteen that had warmed the conspirators after their early boat ride across the cold waters of the bay. A piece of paper, which had been used to carry lead shot, had writing on it which was later shown to belong to Mary McGranaghan of Gortanatra North.

The inquest was held the next day at Milford and, after Kincaid had given his evidence of what he had seen, the coroner, Robert Ramsey, adjourned the hearing for one day so that the results of the post-mortems would be available. Dr Osborne of Milford, who had conducted the examinations, paid tribute in the witness box to the help he had been given by a colleague, Dr Dunlop of Letterkenny. He described the shot found in Leitrim's shattered left shoulder and arm but said that the fatal wound was on the top of his head. He found thirty-three wounds in Buchanan's right arm and chest and assumed that with such trauma death would have been instantaneous. The only wound on Makim's body was the single wound behind the ear which caused a lethal brain haemorrhage. The jury's verdict was reported in the *Londonderry Journal*:

> That the deceased Earl of Leitrim and Charles Buchanan came to their deaths by some persons unknown to the jury and they further pointed out that the Earl of Leitrim's death was hastened by blows upon his head by some

> heavy weapon. Both the late Earl and the car-driver met
> their deaths in the townland of Woodquarter, the 2nd of
> April, 1878. That the deceased John Makim died of an
> effusion of blood on the brain caused by great excitement
> and a gunshot wound on his head behind the left ear.

Reaction was typical of its sources. *The Times* of London feared another outbreak of disorder. The *Londonderry Journal* in its editorial for 3 April called it 'a terrible blot on the character of the people of the County of Donegal, and of the people of Ireland generally'. In their detailed account of the event they noted:

> It is generally supposed in the district that agrarian
> motives prompted the authors of the dastardly outrage.
> For some years past the relations existing between Lord
> Leitrim and his tenantry have been anything but amicable,
> and it is well-known that at various periods since the
> passing of the Land Act his lordship resisted with some
> determination rights which some of the tenants living
> under him believed the law had secured to them.

The *Derry Standard* reminded its readers:

> His name added for a time a new word to the language, for
> when tenants in Donegal were causelessly evicted from
> their holdings in any estate the popular expression was
> that they had been 'Leitrimed'. This one word was
> understood to express the last measure of injustice,
> harshness and desolation.

It also recalled that 'he thought nothing of spending two or three hundred pounds to spite and ruin a tenant who had taken a cart of seaweed in violation of his estate rules'. The *Londonderry Sentinel* published on Thursday, 4 April 1878, insisted justly that 'whatever quarrel existed between the late Earl and his tenantry, there was surely no grudge against the young strange clerk and the driver; but the murderers, acting upon the adage that "dead men tell no tales" carried out their diabolical plot to perfection'. The writer concurred 'with the generous sentiments' of the *Freeman's Journal* that he was not altogether 'a bad man' and chided the *Standard* for portraying 'all the acts of his [Leitrim's] life... in the most malignant terms'. The *Sentinel* also was worried about the murders' effect on the tourist trade.

The landed gentry closed ranks and loudly deprecated the death of their brother, forgetting for the time being that Leitrim was cordially detested by most of them. He was known as the most hated man in Ireland and not just by the native Irish. On the following Sunday Dr McDevitt, Lord Bishop of Raphoe, gave a sermon in St Eunan's Cathedral, denouncing the killing, observing: 'Some might say that Lord Leitrim deserved his fate but "Vengeance is mine," saith the Lord.' It was the correct thing to say but not many agreed. When Leitrim's body arrived at St Michan's Church in Dublin there was the makings of a riot. As reported by the *Freeman's Journal*:

> the crowd closed round the hearse as it approached the graveyard... the mob hooted and groaned, and voices from the worst of them saying, "Out with the old b—", "Lug him out", "Dance on him."

TH Burke, Secretary to the Lord Lieutenant, was authorised by His Grace to offer a reward of £500 'to any person or persons who shall within six months... give such information as shall lead to the arrest of the persons who committed the same'. (Four years later, on 6 May 1882, Burke, as undersecretary to the new liberal Chief Secretary Lord Frederick Cavendish, was himself murdered when he and Lord Cavendish fell victim to the long knives of the 'Invincibles' in Dublin's Phoenix Park.)

Robert Bermingham Clements, Leitrim's nephew, inherited the Leitrim estates as the 4th Earl, despite his uncle's attempt to disinherit him when he cut his brother and two sisters out of his will. Robert offered a reward of £10,000 for effective information but neither his reward nor Burke's were ever claimed. His regime was vastly different from that of his uncle's, modelling himself instead on his kindly grandfather, the 2nd Earl. He restored those evicted to their holdings, in some cases building them new, slated houses.

The usual suspects were rounded up by the highly efficient RIC. On 19 April the *Journal* reported that nine prisoners were examined in the board room of Lifford Jail on 18 April. They were three brothers McGranaghan, Anthony, Bernard and Thomas; their cousins, Anthony and Michael McGranaghan; Patrick and Michael Heraghty, Manus Trainor and Charles McEntaggart. The last two were released without charge when their proximity to the crime scene was explained by their intention to travel out of Donegal — Trainor was on his way to work in Scotland and McEntaggart had a ticket for America. The McGranaghans had all been arrested because of the page torn from Mary McGranaghan's copy book that had been found at the scene. In fact only Michael Heraghty, who had supplied the gun with the red stock and acted as lookout, had any material connection with the killing. The seven were remanded in prison for one week and sat together in the dock at the courthouse in Lifford. There they heard that the Crown would present no evidence against the McGranaghan cousins or against Patrick Heraghty. At the assizes, on 19 July 1878, Michael Heraghty and two of the McGranaghan brothers were found by the jury as having a case to answer. Anthony McGranaghan was eventually discharged.

Before the three remaining defendants could attend the postponed hearing, Michael Heraghty was dead of typhus. He had taken ill on 17 September and died on 12 October. The McGranaghans were also ill. Since the story of Leitrim's end has many elements of myth there is an alternative ending to Heraghty's life. The story goes that another prisoner who had died was substituted for Heraghty, laid in his bed and the death certificate was signed. Meanwhile Heraghty was put in a coffin and taken outside of the jail. He was nursed back to health and emigrated to America. In the coffin a block of wood for weight was wedged with bolts of cloth to prevent movement and there was a nasty moment when Heraghty's 'widow' asked to have the coffin opened. The officiating priest would not permit it and the block of wood was buried with all due ceremony. The story concludes with the information that the whole caper was organised by the Fenians in Dublin.

The Crown had no evidence to offer against the McGranaghans and they were released on indefinite bail after nearly a year in prison. Sheils and McElwee were never arrested and the former survived until 1924. Some locals say that McElwee died of typhus shortly after the killing but others insist that he survived until the twentieth century. Though the rewards offered were substantial no one made any attempt to claim them. Most people in Donegal knew perfectly well what had happened but had no interest in turning informer; such a charge would never be forgiven for a couple of generations at least. As a local ballad, written shortly afterwards, goes, there would be 'no rotten (family) members/From Moville to Aranmore.' Liam Dolan, in his *The Third Earl of Leitrim*, prints a report that was prepared by William Martin, the Sessional Crown Solicitor, and sent to Dublin Castle on 1 July 1880. Martin names 'Michael McElwee of Ballyhoriskey, known as "Mickey Roe", Neal Sheills of Doagmore both in Fannett and Michael Herrighty who was arrested and died in Lifford Gaol.' Therefore the authorities knew but could by no means prove who ended the life of the hated landlord. As Sub-Inspector Bailey told the magistrate in Lifford on 18 April 1878, the constabulary was experiencing considerable difficulty in obtaining evidence in the face of a very tight-lipped and hostile local population.

The memorial cross set up in Kindrum in 1960 named these men with pride and suggested that they had ended the tyranny of landlordism, which is surely exaggerated. The undoubted tyranny of landlordism was ended rather by such events of the

Great Famine, the British liberal conscience, as personified in such people as Gladstone, the force of public opinion, the Land League and the series of land acts. The process had already began in Leitrim's lifetime and his savage killing, if anything, delayed the ultimate solution. The old adage that bad cases make bad law applies here. Leitrim was the worst of cases, a slur on the name of a tolerable family. One can understand how his tenants were driven to extremes by his arrogance and bloody-mindedness. However, he died well and one cannot help feeling sorry for Buchanan and Makim, a clear case of guilt by association. The old toast, 'Here's to the hand that made the ball/That shot Lord Leitrim in Donegal', may not be heard much nowadays but the name of William Sydney Clements, 3rd Earl of Leitrim, lives on in infamy.

6
NORA AND ARTHUR

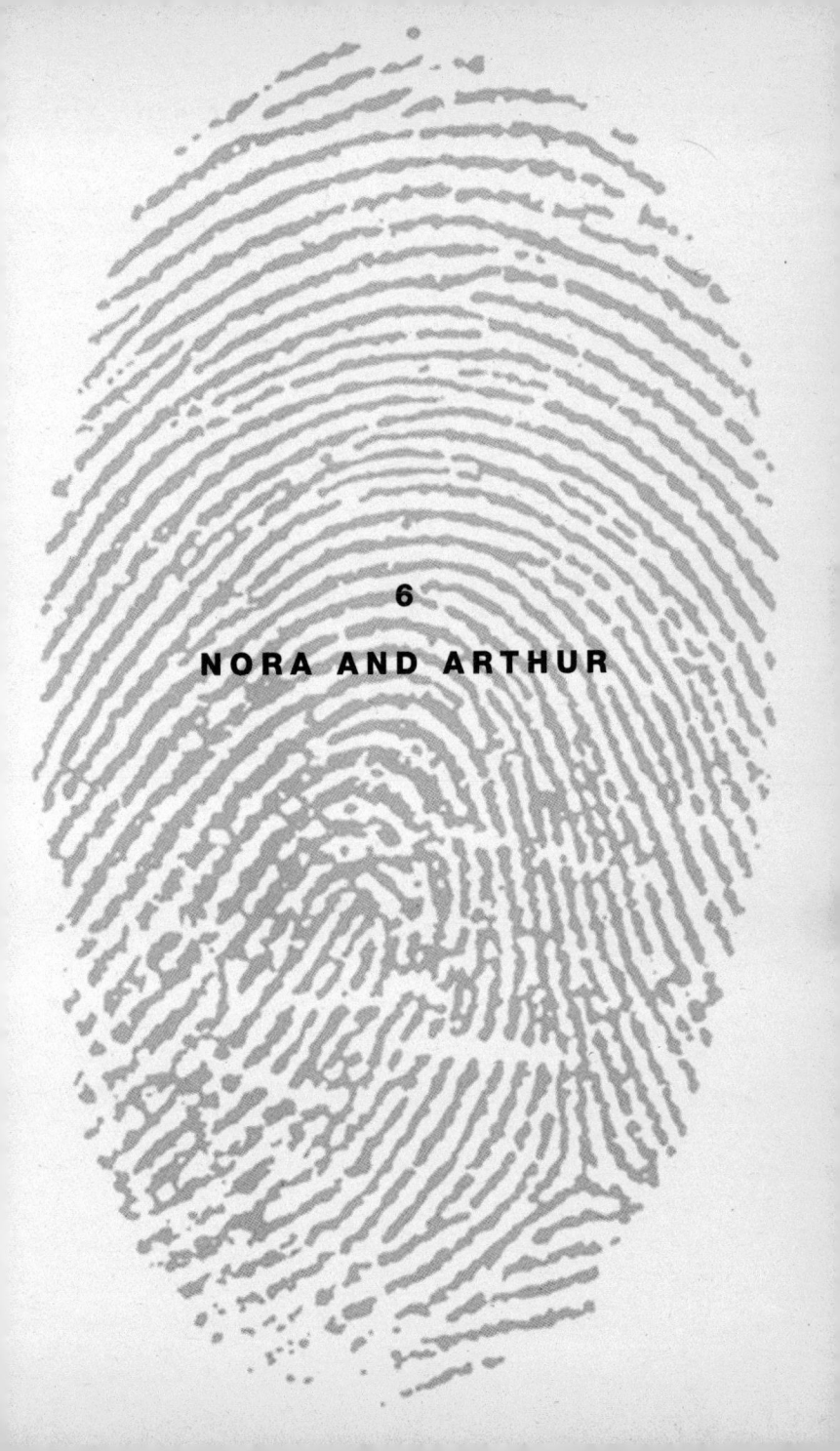

THE NOTION OF A SUICIDE PACT made by unhappy lovers has a long and romantic history. It is substantially different from the 'domestic', when a partner murders his soul-mate in a rage and then — horrified — commits suicide. The idea that some couples prefer death to separation or feel that the world is too cruel a place has given rise to many 'Lovers' Leaps'. East Sussex's Beachy Head became such a popular place for these couples that it now has health and safety regulations governing its approach. Bridges too, notably any one of those to Manhattan from other parts of New York City or San Francisco's Golden Gate — which at 1,500 has three times as many suicide couples as Beachy Head — have now got barriers to prevent this last final act of desperation/defiance. These measures belong to the late twentieth and twenty-first centuries; in the nineteenth century there were few physical restrictions but possibly more obstacles for young couples to negotiate.

Belfast has always looked to Cave Hill and its parkland as a civic amenity. In June 1795 the United Irishmen — Wolfe Tone, Samuel Neilsen, Henry Joy McCracken and Thomas Russell — spent forty-eight hours on top of the 1,182 foot cliff at Mac Art's fort, or Napoleon's nose as it later was called, before Tone sailed for America, vowing 'never to desist in our efforts until we have subverted the authority of England over our country and asserted our independence'. It used to be infamous for its raucous Easter festivity but thanks to nineteenth-century church ministers fulminating about the free-for-all, the drinking and fornicating that characterised the Easter rout, the festival all but disappeared. However, it remained a favourite place for picnics and lovers' trysts before the advent of the zoo.

Then, in 1890, it was the scene of a death pact, whether romantic or not remains questionable. The *Belfast News Letter* of Thursday, 13 March 1890, carried the account under the triple headlines: 'Terrible Tragedy near Belfast; Murder and Suicide; Romantic and Sensational Details.' That morning, 'the stillness and solitude of Cave Hill were broken by the report of four shots'. It was a quiet place, then 'near Belfast', far from the clang of the shipbuilders' hammers in the 'Island' and the other noises of Ireland's 'Linenopolis'. The land was mainly used for farming and there were stone quarries supplying material for the new roads that the city's spread required. At about 9am Francis Hyde, a farmer, was surprised to hear a fusillade of three revolver shots followed by a fourth after a short interval. The reports came from a natural hollow near the quarries and Hyde could see a wisp of smoke rising from the spot. In some trepidation he made his way to the hollow which was a favourite spot for courting, though hardly at 9am on a raw March morning.

What he found upset him considerably; a young couple lay there cradled in each other's arms, the man with his head on the woman's breast. Hyde thought that she was dead but, because he could hear what sounded like soft groans, thought that the man was still, if only barely, alive. He ran for help to the only house in the vicinity. Henry Boyle had heard the shots and then, seeing his neighbour run across the fields, quickly opened his door and went to meet him. He accompanied Hyde back to the hollow and confirmed his first impressions. The woman, lying facing the city, had three bullet holes on her left temple, a little above her ear. Her eyes and forehead were covered by a handkerchief and the man's head was similarly masked. He had a gunshot wound on his right temple while the left side of his face lay on the woman's chest. A revolver lay beside them and both were covered by a silk umbrella, the handle of which was caught in a piece of elastic that stretched from the woman's hat to a button on her jacket. The hat was in fashionable imitation of a sailor's round cap.

They had tied the handkerchiefs round each other's eyes and opened the umbrella to make a kind of rudimentary shelter for their ghastly ritual. The woman was unquestionably dead, a fact confirmed by a Doctor Newett who arrived with police from Ligoniel. (Ligoniel was then a mill village on the outskirts of the city, retaining the anglicised form of its old Gaelic name, *Lag an Aoil* — lime-hollow — the title coming from the proximity of limestone quarries.) Sergeant Farrell and two RIC constables had been summoned by Boyle from the nearest police barracks. Hyde had been left reluctantly with the bodies and was visibly relieved when Constable Gibson took his place. The Ligoniel coroner, Dr Mussen, ordered the woman's body to be conveyed to the village for an inquest. A cart was commandeered for the man and he was rushed to the Royal Hospital in Frederick Street, off York Street (the forerunner of the Royal Victoria that was transferred to its present site in 1903). There he died, as the newspaper put it, 'succumbed shortly after his admission, notwithstanding the efforts and skill of Dr. Wheeler and his staff'.

It was clear that the man 'first took away the life of his sweetheart and then destroyed himself'. His name, it transpired, was George Arthur. He lived with his parents in 150 Nelson Street, quite close to the hospital, and worked as a clerk at the office of Messrs G&J Burns at 49 Queen's Square, off Victoria Street. The woman was identified as Nora Tattersell, a maidservant in the house of James Best of 3 Clarence Place. They had been seeing each other for several months but there was some barrier to their marrying, the precise nature of which was never revealed. They used to meet once a week but he managed to turn up at the railings outside her master's house a few times a day. Best spoke glowingly about Nora's virtues as a maidservant. He found her 'honest, attractive and hardworking, and her relations with the family were always of the most harmonious character'. The one slightly odd thing about her concerned her relations with her own family. She never wrote to them nor ever went home on a visit. Best was concerned when Nora did not return from an intended visit to Carrickfergus 'on private business'. The reporter who interviewed Best was told that he had received a telegram but did not reveal its contents nor would the police give any details about it.

Best knew nothing of her whereabouts until news filtered down of the tragedy, genuinely shocking him. George Arthur's family were not too upset when he was late. He occasionally stayed extra hours to clear a build-up of work, though at the inquest his brother Ezekiel said that they had sat up till nearly midnight waiting for him to come home. Since Arthur had died in Belfast the inquest was held by Dr Dill, the city coroner, in the extern department of the Frederick Street Royal at 8pm on the evening of the tragedy. Ezekiel related how he had gone to the mortuary on the instructions of a policeman who came to the Arthur house to tell them the dire news at midday: [He] 'further said that the young lady was dead and that if I wanted to see my brother alive I should go at once to the Royal Hospital... I then proceeded to the hospital with the Constable, and saw my brother who was then in the deadhouse, having died in the meantime.' Arthur must have been taken to the mortuary just a short time before because there had been no attempt to clean him. Ezekiel found that his brother's face was covered with dried blood but he could see no sign of a wound. It was then about 12.25pm.

Questioned about a possible relationship he said that he knew from the day before that George had a lady friend. He had bumped into him about 5.10pm on the Tuesday evening in York Street; Ezekiel was going home to Nelson Street and they chatted briefly for a few minutes. George told Ezekiel that he was going to meet his sweetheart but did not say where. Ezekiel could not remember whether he said 'girl' or 'sweetheart'. It is clear that poor Ezekiel was both shocked by the tragedy and the awfulness of the inquest; nothing else can explain the stiltedness and attempted grandness of his witness statements. He 'proceeded' to the hospital, for example, using the formal vocabulary of police officers in the witness box.

He had to answer questions from individual jurymen as well as the coroner, and County Inspector Brownrigg and Detective Inspector McArdle, of the RIC, who represented the constabulary. James McDermott, the foreman of the jury, asked him about the revolver and how it came into his brother's possession but he could not answer: 'I never knew him to carry firearms.' Another juror, a Mr Jones, wondered if George had been drinking. Ezekiel replied that he was completely sober when he talked to him and that he was not in the habit of drinking alcohol. Inspector McArdle asked him about George's job and was told that he been with Messrs Burns for about a year and a half, earning eighteen shillings a week, paid monthly, all of which he gave to his mother. He had not mentioned anything about his girlfriend to his parents but Ezekiel said that they would not have raised any objection to his marrying. When the revolver was produced he did not recognise it; he had only seen handguns in shop windows. His evidence concluded when shown a letter by McArdle which he confirmed to be in his brother's handwriting.

The next witness was Francis Hyde, who appeared excited with the attention. He repeated the story of how he had found the bodies and provided more detail that he had given previously to the *News Letter* reporter: 'I reside in the townland of Ballyaghaghan, at the Cave Hill and am employed as a labourer by Mr Lowry.' He deposed, as the report rather formally put it, that he was working in one of his fields at 7am (in his earlier report he said 9am) 'when I heard three or four shots and saw smoke about three or four perches distant'. He thought it odd to hear shots at that season of year. He went to the roadway and 'observed a man lying in the corner of a field with an opened umbrella over him.' He fetched Henry Boyle who lived nearby and the two of them went to the scene. Boyle rather masterfully pocketed the gun and dispatched Hyde to Ligoniel. However,

Hyde refused to go — many people at the time were a little bit uneasy about going anywhere near a police barracks — but said he was happy to stay at the scene until the police arrived.

Sergeant John Farrell was on duty in Ligoniel police barracks that morning when Henry Boyle had arrived 'at a quarter past nine'. He had little new in the way of information to add but certain details like the opened umbrella, the silk handkerchiefs used as blindfolds and the fact that Nora Tattersell still wore a sailor hat, gained a kind of iconic strength. He described how he had searched George Arthur's clothing and found a box of pinfire cartridges, which corresponded in every particular with the revolver he had 'assisted to unload' earlier. The most interesting piece of evidence presented by the sergeant was the reading aloud of Arthur's letter which he had promised the coroner he would read when giving his evidence. It was addressed to the editor of the *Evening Telegraph* (later the *Belfast Telegraph*) and read as follows:

> No one must ever blame dear Nora for what has occurred. It has not been her fault. We love each other but there have been certain things in the past which prevent our union and by mutual agreement we have consented to die rather than continue to live in this weary world. I am sorry to take her life but also there is no alternative. God forgive me. Never was there such a good tender-hearted angel born in this world before. I wish, my dear mother, that you knew more of her, you could better understand but I cannot explain any further. Do not think for one moment that she is to blame for the step I am taking now. No. She would die to save me one moment's pains and I would do the same for her. Forgive me mother, father, brothers and sisters. A long farewell. God bless you all. And darling Nora and I. My dear darling Nora, I am happy in the thought that we die together, welcome is death, with you, dear. The Coroner's jury may return their usual verdict of temporary insanity, but I am not even temporarily insane;

NORA AND ARTHUR

on the contrary, I am clothed in my right mind. Farewell Bod, Hugh, Johnny and all the rest of my long-respected pals. Many a jolly time we had together but all's well that ends well, and the end has come for me and I hope it will be well. Nora darling — last but not least, my own lovely darling — farewell until we meet on the other side of the river. You remember what I wrote you once before, dear, in the words of Byron (I think) —

'I cannot lose a world for thee
But would not lose thee for the world.'

God forgive me, and bless my own dear Nora.

George

P.S. — There is too much work for me at those ledger accounts.

The same envelope also contained the following:

A fear lest one should utter
    Rude words to pain some heart
Or do an action thoughtlessly
    To make the teardrops start

A curbing of the temper,
    A bridling of the tongue,
When for the good of other souls
    Will make the old seem young.

Then, more than faultless features
    And more that golden hair
Regard the gift of graciousness,
    O, maiden sweet and fair,

That, when you go forth daily,
    The thought of every mind
Will be she is so beautiful,
    Because she is so kind.

True, what is youth and beauty,
    Bright eyes and tresses fair,

Without the gift of graciousness?
    A gift, alas, too rare.

But well, too, it becometh
    This tender thoughtful grace
This courtesy to all around
    The plainest form and face.

The gentle thought for others,
    Forgetting self awhile;
The willingness to minister
    And human woe beguile.

The question asked in kindness
    The answer kindly given,
Will give the human countenance
    A beauty born of heaven.

The poetry was hardly Byronic; it was a typical piece of 'improving' Victorian verse and it is hard to see why Arthur should have included it with his suicide note. Its bland sententiousness seems a strange bedfellow with the touching last letter. With the lapse of so many years — more than 116 — it is hard to know what its significance was for the blighted lovers. Perhaps they used to read verse to each other; the piece may have been a favourite with Nora or it may have been part of Arthur's own repertoire. The search of Arthur's clothing also yielded two more letters, one 'written in a female hand'. It was headed '3 Clarence Place' and dated 11 December 1889. It indicates the existence of some impediment to their future happiness and though written three months before what the papers insisted in calling the 'romantic tragedy', a psychologist might well find in it the source of later events:

Dear George —
I am sorry for fretting you last night. If you knew the state of my mind you would forgive me for getting into such a temper. It makes me so miserable to see you wasting your

time coming down to see me when I know I am anything but worthy of you. There is a great barrier which my feelings prevent me telling you either by word or letter, but some day, perhaps, you will know. I won't go out on a wet night again, as I got cold last night, and I have been suffering from neuralgia all day. Like a good child don't come down before Friday night, about 9.30 p.m. I was greatly pleased to see you lately so steady. I must now say good-bye, as I have a heater in the fire, and if I don't go soon it will melt. — Your fond

                                                    Nora

Love is a dream,
Sad is the waking,
Sunshine and sorrow must ever be.
Love is a dream;
Oh! would it last for ever
For life is so hard,
And love is so sweet.

Perhaps this tailpiece was the beginning of the compiling of their personal anthology. Maybe Nora wrote the verse herself and although hardly original it was clearly deeply felt. The nature barrier to the couple's marriage was never discovered though rumours circulated that perhaps Nora had been married before. One gets the impression that she was the stronger of the two. The other letter written to her on the Tuesday, before they died, could have been a supplement to the 'farewell' letter. George may have intended to hand it to Nora when they met for the final act or else he read it aloud to her, which would explain it being in his pocket when their bodies were found. There is a sense that the strain of what he contemplated was beginning to get to him. Perhaps he felt impatient about how slowly time was passing until the terrible moment and anticipated by letter what he should say when they met. If, as his brother believed, he drank very little as a rule it should not have been necessary to make promises to her about keeping off liquor and, as Dr

Johnson once said about the prospect of imminent death, it concentrates the mind wonderfully. Nora seemed to have found it necessary to admonish her lover from time to time. The remark about his own wickedness spurs a different run of speculation and the final flourish seems a little bit melodramatic. The letter was written from his workplace in Queen's Square.

> My own darling —
> I have come into the office simply to drop you a few lines. I do not wish to stay very long, so that I can only say a very few words to you. I have kept my promise to you, and have not tasted any drink today, so that my head is perfectly clear, and I am very happy in the knowledge that we both die together. Be cheerful, darling, and keep up your spirits until I come round at seven o'clock. How I long for the time when I see you again. I wonder will it be for the last time. No, it cannot be so, for truly the good Lord will let us meet again in the next world. I will pray to Him for you, Nora, but I cannot do so for myself; I have been so wicked. God bless you, my own bonnie — God bless you.
> Yours true till death
> George

There was rapt attention from those present while Sergeant Farrell read out the letters. When he finished he pointed out that he still didn't know where the revolver or cartridges came from. 'I found likewise three shillings and some coppers and a few Christmas cards.' A rather odd piece of information was that he had found a small quantity of his hair in her possession. One would have expected the opposite, that he had a lock of her hair with him. It is not clear when exactly Farrell searched Nora's body. Perhaps the *News Letter* reporter got it wrong. Farrell's evidence concluded with his statement that he had the body of the young man brought to the Royal Hospital where he died on admission. This was confirmed by Dr WA Wheeler, resident surgeon at the hospital:

> George Arthur was admitted to the hospital at a quarter to twelve o'clock today. He was absolutely unconscious and in a dying state, and there was a small wound on the right temple, which appeared to be a bullet wound. He never recovered consciousness and died a few moments before twelve o'clock. The wound was such as could have been easily self-inflicted.

Dr Dill, the coroner, was still anxious to prove that the demon drink had played a significant role in the affair and had Ezekiel Arthur recalled to the witness stand. He reaffirmed his original statement that his brother took a little drink in moderation. He also said that George had not missed work at any time during the previous fortnight. Turning to the jury Dill reminded them that they were not to concern themselves with the young woman's death, as it would be investigated by the county coroner. Not unexpectedly the jury took little time to reach their verdict:

> That the said George Arthur, on the 12th day of March, 1890, in the Royal Hospital in the city of Belfast, came to his death from the effects of a bullet wound; and so the jurors do say that the said George Arthur did commit suicide.

The newspaper account ended with the terse sentence: 'The inquiry then terminated.'

The *News Letter* of the following day, Friday, 14 March, concluded the story with more than three full columns in tiny 8-point print under the sentimental lead: 'The Romantic Tragedy on the Cave Hill'. The paper admitted that very few additional facts had to be recorded 'in connection with the sad murder and suicide which took place on the Cave Hill on Wednesday morning, and little or no light has been thrown upon the sad and tragic occurrence which is at present almost the sole topic of conversation in the city'. The respectable family of George Arthur had the sympathy of all while the efforts to trace the relatives of Nora Tattersell had met with no success in spite of the endeavours of the police and many telegrams sent to places where she might have been known. Some said that she had a brother in the Dublin Metropolitan Police Force, the elite constabulary that was founded in 1836.

It is hard nowadays to believe that a person could retain such privacy and mystery. James Best told the police that she had come to him from Portadown. Joseph Douglas, her employer there, said that before working for him she spent six months in the household of the Rev Robert Jamison. Douglas said that 'she had performed her duties very satisfactorily, but she appeared to him to be a very peculiar girl'. This, as the *News Letter* reporter wrote, 'tallies to a great extent with the opinion expressed by Mr Best'. He said that she was of a nervous and excitable disposition but had always given the greatest attention and care to her duties until some time ago, which, continued the report, 'would seem to correspond with the period when the unhappy attachment with Arthur commenced'.

It seemed that she originally came from Dublin and her acquaintances noted her 'decided southern accent or brogue', then more common in the second city than later. Inevitably, with so little factual information available, all kinds of theories began to develope. One interesting speculation suggested that she was the wife of a 'sea-captain', which might be the dreaded secret that she could not yet reveal even to George Arthur.

On the day of her death, while her inquest was being held, a man by the name of Robert Templeton, of 103 Grosvenor Road, went to the police and said that a man called James Tattersell, perhaps a brother of the dead woman, had lived for two or three years as a lodger with John Livesey of Albert Place, off Donegall Pass. Templeton insisted that Nora had a strong resemblance to him. The paper described her as 'a woman of regular and intelligent features' but with one drawback: 'one of her eyes — the right one — was completely blind, having been injured some years ago, it is stated, in the course of a practical joke.' An operation performed to try to restore the sight had been unsuccessful but the defect did not affect her personal appearance, 'which was that of a respectable, educated and intelligent woman'. The police continued their enquiries about Nora's family but her reticence about her background made their task virtually impossible. Typical of the mystery with which she surrounded herself was the fact that she tore the word 'Tattersell' from the flyleaf of her Bible, leaving only 'Nora' on the page, though it is not known when this excision took place.

The inquest was held on the Thursday, the day after their bodies had been retrieved from the hallow. The police hoped that it might encourage some relative to appear. As we have seen, the only information came from Robert Templeton and by then the trail had gone cold. As the reporter put it, 'the past life of the unfortunate woman still remains to all intents and purposes a sealed book'. Friday's paper gave more information about George Arthur that had not been revealed at his inquest on the Wednesday, the day of his death. His weekly wage was stated by Andrew Gibson, the office manager in G&J Burns, to be £1 rather than the eighteen shillings indicated by his brother. Gibson also elucidated the remark about the ledgers in the postscript to his last letter to Nora. Arthur had asked to tackle the ledger accounts with the hope of promotion, should he prove competent. More details of his working life were given by Gibson. He had received a second increase of salary within three months; his office hours were based upon different schedules on alternate weeks. One week he worked from 9am till 6pm with an hour and a quarter off for dinner, the next week he worked from 9am till 8pm with the same dinner leave and an hour for tea. He was free from 2pm on alternate Saturdays. Any overtime was voluntary, as he and other clerks covered for a colleague who had had to leave because of ill health four months previously, but whose job was being kept for him and his full salary was being paid. It was quite enlightened for the time.

Before joining G&J Burns he had served his apprenticeship as a clerk in the office of the Belfast and Northern Counties Railway Company, the forerunner of the LMS (NCC) that still runs to

Derry as Translink. Arthur then joined the Army Medical Staff Corps but was invalided out. (His competence in firearms probably dates from that period.) He returned to Belfast and was unemployed for a considerable number of months until Gibson was induced to give him the post of junior clerk. He was a faithful clerk and generally popular in the Burns office. He does not strike one as a man bent upon murder and suicide. The character delineated here may have been that of the time before he fell in love with the one-eyed girl with the southern brogue.

Since Nora's death had taken place outside the city in the county the inquest was held by Dr Mussen, the coroner for South Antrim. It took place at 10am on Thursday, 13 March in the public house of JJ O'Hare in Ligoniel. County Inspector Brownrigg was again present and Head Constable Wilson was there in default of DI Fleury who was absent through illness. JJ O'Hare was chairman of the jury and he personally viewed the body. The first witness was again Francis Hyde who told his story without any further elaboration except that he warned Henry Boyle, his neighbour, 'Don't go too quick for he might shoot you,' and named the place as 'a hollow in Lowry's plantation'. Boyle largely corroborated Hyde's account, stating that he had taken possession of the revolver that was not in the man's hand but on the ground between the two bodies. He said that there was blood on the woman's jacket but that it had come from the wound in the man's temple. A juror asked Boyle if he had heard anything before the noise of the shooting and he replied that he had been out early in the morning but had seen no one going to or from the plantation. To the coroner's next question he replied that he knew neither one of the couple nor had he ever seen either of them before, to his knowledge.

Nora's employer, James Best, was next in the dock. The coroner commiserated with him on the shock of the occurrence and began by asking him about the spelling of Nora's surname. As to Nora's age, Best thought she was about twenty-three and she had worked in his house for about a year and a half. She

NORA AND ARTHUR

appeared to be a quiet industrious girl. She had left 3 Clarence Place on Monday evening about 7.30pm or shortly after and he had not seen her alive again. She told him that she was going to Carrickfergus 'to look after a situation'. She had been keeping company with the young man, George Arthur, since the previous October. Asked if she had other boyfriends Best said he was aware of another friend, a Highlander called Ramsey, who was a sergeant or corporal in the army but had since left or was discharged because of ill-health. She became acquainted with Arthur when Ramsey was leaving on the return boat to Scotland. It had not escaped Best's knowledge that Arthur often appeared near the house to hope for a word with Nora but Best did not know him sufficiently well to identify the body as he always waited round the corner.

Head Constable Wilson asked the obvious question: 'Did you notice anything peculiar in the deceased woman's disposition latterly?' Best answered that she was an extremely nervous and highly excitable girl and he hadn't noticed anything extraordinary. Wilson then asked about a telegram that Best had received, which, it was believed, had come from Arthur. It read: 'Nora bids you goodbye. Look under her pillow; do not be too hard on her when you know.' Best said that the telegram had arrived about twenty-five minutes to eleven. (Telegrams in those days supplied the deficit of the lack of telephones and the young messengers with their shiny buttons, round hats and solid-tired bicycles worked late into the night.) When Best read the telegram he and his wife went to Nora's bedroom and retrieved a note that was hidden under her pillow. He then took the note to the police station. The note was written on an old envelope turned inside out and read:

To Mrs. Best.

Nora

Forgive me for what I have done. But I could live no

> longer. Burn everything Belong [sic] to me. Don't trouble
> to look for me. I think you did not act just to me. But I
> forgive you now.
> When you get this I will
> Be no more.

One of the jurymen asked Best if he knew anything of the family of the girl but he knew 'nothing whatever', aside from Nora letting it be known conversationally, in Clarence Place, that she had a brother in the metropolitan force and that her father had also been in the DMP but had been killed a few years ago. He repeated that no papers came with her to his house though he knew that her previous employer was Joseph Douglas of Portadown. Another juror wanted to know if Mrs Best had had any occasion to reprimand Miss Tattersell, as explanation for the maidservant's charge that she did not act justly to her. Best defended his wife saying that she was more indulgent towards her than to any other servant he had ever employed. However she had not been 'attending to her duties the way she had done previously' and had been given notice to leave on 1 April. Nora had pleaded with her and promised to do better.

Sergeant John Farrell was next to be cross-examined. His evidence repeated all he had said at Arthur's inquest in the Royal Hospital. Wilson asked if he had had any success in discovering 'the history of the deceased'. Farrell said that he had checked with the DMP about the existence of an officer called Tattersell but there had never been anyone of that name in the force. He also wired the Portadown police but had not yet received an answer. O'Hara, the jury foreman, wondered if Nora might be pregnant but was reassured when Dr Newett said there was absolutely no evidence of that. For that reason it was decided not to hold a post-mortem. He also confirmed that any one of the wounds would have been sufficient to cause death and that they could not have been self-inflicted. Summing up, the coroner asked the jury to take cognisance of all the evidence that they had heard and added, perhaps a little unwisely, that in his opinion the circumstances all pointed to the conclusion that all the shots had been discharged by the hand of George Arthur. That was also the opinion of the jury, for their verdict read:

> ...George Arthur on Tuesday the 12th day of March, in the year of our Lord 1890 at Ballyaghaghan, in the parish of Shankill, in the County of Antrim, feloniously did kill and murder Nora Tattersell, by firing three bullets into her left temple.

In fact they got they day wrong. The killing took place on the Wednesday morning.

When the inquest was over John Arthur, another brother of George's, said that he thought the bodies of George and Nora should be buried together and he would make all the necessary arrangements for the interment. The coroner said he was sure that Mr Best would raise no objections. They were buried in the City Cemetery on the Falls Road on the Friday morning. The funeral procession went from York Street to the Crumlin Road, and by Agnes Street and Northumberland Street to the Falls. George's body was taken from the hospital by hearse and Nora's from the funeral parlour of Leonard Braithwaite, close by in Talbot Street, off Donegall Street. The streets were lined with sightseers and behind the hearses walked the father and brothers of George Arthur, and Andrew Gibson, accompanied by other employees of G&J Burns. George was buried first and then Nora's coffin was placed in the same grave.

There was a characteristically grim sermon, bristling with Victorian admonition, by the Rev John Spence, a minister from the Mariners Church (where George worshipped). He first read Psalm 90 with its emphasis on the wrath of Jehovah and the transience of life. His text for the sermon was Hebrews: 9; 27, the chilling, 'It is appointed unto men once to die, but after this the judgement.' He chided many who had come 'influenced by a morbid sentimentality'. He did not blame 'the Press or the members of the Press... for if there was not an unholy, base, sensual thirst for such things, the news would not be supplied'. His peroration was not unexpected:

> ...ask yourselves the questions, 'Am I living a Christian life?' 'Am I walking in the way to heaven?' 'Are my sins forgiven; am I ready to die?' 'Am I prepared to meet my God?' Then you will have learned the lessons of the day, and God, who alone can, will have turned a curse into a blessing, and made that which is a terrible calamity — the result undoubtedly of forgetting God and losing sight of him — into a blessing to you and to me.

There was no more than a perfunctory word of comfort for the grieving Arthur family and no reference to the two lovers. After the report of Spencer's sermon the paper's account of the funerals concluded with a sentence in keeping with what the mourners had just heard: 'The melancholy proceedings then terminated, and the large assemblage dispersed to their homes.'

It was not quite the end of the story. The police enquiries as to the biography of Nora Tattersell continued but produced 'no practical result'. Confirmation of her service with the Rev Mr Jamison of Portadown came with the further information that she had worked for him while he lived in Wexford. Jamison told the police that no member of Nora Tattersell's family was at present in Ireland. 'Her mother was married a second time and went to live in England many years since. Deceased had no correspondence with her. She has an aunt, whose maiden name was Hart, living in Midleton, County Cork. She [the aunt] is married to a cooper.' Jamison did not know the married name of the aunt but believed that she was the only relative she had in Ireland. The *News Letter* reported that a telegram sent to the police in Midleton 'elicited the reply that they were unable to discover any such person as the aunt notwithstanding a vigorous search with that view'. The paper also reported that they had received a letter from Mr J Livesey of 79 Dublin Road stating that a man named Tattersell was a personal friend of his and had often visited his house but had never lived with him, and that it was a mistake to suppose that he was any relation of the deceased woman. The paper concluded its coverage of the funerals with: 'The inquiries as to the whereabouts of her friends are, therefore, at a standstill, and it is questionable if the mystery of her past life will ever be elucidated.'

Ten days later on Monday, 24 March, the *Northern Whig* published a piece of news from Newry, dated Saturday night. The report indicated that a Mrs McCarthy Connor, the wife of a local solicitor, had given relevant information about Nora. The 'romantic' story had become news countrywide. It seemed that the dead woman used the name Hart and had lived with her sister Jessie Tattersell, who was a nurse/superintendent in a Cork hospital. Nora had been treated there for the eye injury that had left her blind in one eye. Mrs Connor then lived in 9 North Street in the southern city. Five years earlier nineteen-year-old Nora worked as a general servant at that address. (She still was causing confusion about her past.) During her time in North Street she revealed that her real name was Tattersell but her claim that she had worked as a nurse at Shandy Hall was false. She also told of her father being in the DMP and his death during a riot in Dublin. This we have seen was fantasy; there was no record of an officer called Tattersell. The injury to her left eye had left her sight generally defective and since she could not carry out the duties of a housemaid to her own satisfaction Mrs Connor had used her as a children's nurse.

She must have had some nursing experience because she successfully worked in the village of Coachford, on the River Lee, twenty miles west of Cork, as a carer for the wife of the Rev Mr Gollock, who was an invalid. Mrs Connor lost track of her after she left Coachford but later heard that she worked at the Curragh and subsequently in Dublin. Mrs Connor also confirmed that Nora's mother had remarried after her husband's death and had gone to live in England, and the twelve-year-old Nora had gone to live with her grandmother. It was from there that she went to Cork to be with her sister Jessie and later worked for her in North Street. Mrs Connor confirmed that she was very beautiful in spite of her defect, which was scarcely noticeable anyway. She also said that considering her position in life she was very well educated and had a sweet singing voice that showed professional training. She, like James Best, remarked upon her excitable temperament, talking often of the day she had seen her father carried in dead and berating herself for unkindness shown to her grandmother while she was alive. In fact she and her grandparents lived 'on affectionate terms'. Mrs Connor thought that it was an overactive imagination that caused the outbursts of grief for her dead father and grandmother.

The mystery of the dark secret that she could not reveal even to her lover remains, as does the reason for the pact to end it all. George's language — 'weary world', for example — seems a little contrived, perhaps it was the result of coaching by Nora. It was probably she who first suggested death as the only solution to their misery. Motive remains a puzzle; the theory that their difference in class was a factor isn't convincing. She was clearly better educated than he was and even in the straitened conditions of employment her possibility of self-improvement was if anything better than his. The position of a junior clerk, however ambitious, was socially not much above that of a domestic servant and they had a reputation for marrying RIC constables! There were many women in similar employment and the lucky ones learned a great deal about life in grander houses. Some went on to become housekeepers and even owners of bed-and-breakfast establishments or small hotels. At the level at which they lived it was possible to move socially up, and in some unlucky cases down.

In that pre-antibiotic age there was no cure for syphilis and even the lesser venereal disease of gonorrhoea could cause blindness, acute arthritis and illness in any children born of an infected mother. Might this have been the reason for the death pact? All such speculation remains tantalisingly frustrating; we simply have not enough information. Nora had undoubtedly an imagination that tended to get over-heated and she seems to have been prone to depressions. George was the true romantic, susceptible to the charms of the woman whom he tried to catch a glimpse of most days by being outside her house during his lunch hour. Love, they say, makes the world go round; it may also make the world seem a place of triviality and better lost. We just don't know. It is probably pure coincidence that fourteen months earlier, on 30 January 1889, the bodies of Crown Prince Rudolf of Austria, the emperor's only son, and his mistress, Baroness Marie Vetsera, were found victims of a suicide pact in southern Austria. It caused a sensation; there was no one in the direct line to become ruler of the Austro-Hungarian Empire and the history of Europe for the next hundred years was irrevocably changed. The 'romantic' story of the prince and the commoner unable to live together openly and choosing to die rather than face life without one other caught the imagination of the world, affecting even provincial Belfast. Perhaps the impressionable Nora took it as a royal precedent and persuaded the malleable George to see it as the solution to the problems that oppressed them.

The truth is that we will never know the full story. Nora was too clever a fantasist ever to reveal the truth about her past. One other question remains to puzzle us. We know that George had arranged to meet her at 7pm on the Tuesday evening and in spite of Frank Hyde's contradictory evidence we can assume that it was at 7am the following morning that they died. How did they spend their last twelve conscious hours? Maybe like another pair of star-crossed lovers, Antony and Cleopatra in Shakespeare's play, they had 'one other gaudy night'. Dawn would have just been breaking on that Wednesday in March, 116 years ago, when poor George Arthur bound the silk handkerchief round the eyes of his beloved Nora and fired the three shots into her brain. He wasn't quite so lucky with his own suicide; he lived to feel the pain of more than just separation. It can be confidently assumed that the chief dynamism came from Nora but the belief in the world well lost was probably George's. Press coverage was kind and many of those who lined the streets for the funeral did so out of a kind of solidarity. All the world loves a lover and two like George and Nora wrung real sympathy out of ordinary people. Not unexpectedly it is Nora who is nominally remembered. For many years after, the hollow in Lowry's plantation was known as 'Nora's Grave'.

7
CONELL BOYLE

THE AREA OF WEST DONEGAL known as the Rosses lies, as one of its native authors, Fionn Mac Cumhaill, wrote, 'between the two sea-inlets, Gweedore and Gweebarra'. The name of the region in Irish is *Rosa*, which means 'headlands' or 'promontories', and a glance at a map will prove the relevance of the name. Nowadays it is famous as a tourist area with magnificent beaches, a golf course on Cruit Island with striking views, an airport at Carrickfinn, several Irish colleges and celebrated as the birthplace of the singer Daniel O'Donnell, who was born in Kincasslagh. The land is generally harsh with fertile pieces won by hard graft from rock-strewn whin-covered terrain and dotted at every turn with lakes of varying sizes among the bogs. There are many new houses and a general air of prosperity as befits the new Ireland. In 1898, however, things were vastly different. There were no fine bungalows with beautifully tended gardens. Instead for most people there was mere subsistence living in a harsh part of Ireland that had changed little for centuries.

The improvements in communication that characterised most of the country were only beginning to impact on this remote area. The Strabane–Glenties branch of the County Donegal Railway had an important stop at Fintown which was in a sense the gateway to the Rosses from the south and it was to there that migrant workers from the area walked to catch the train that would take them to twice-yearly hiring fairs in Strabane or as the first part of the journey to Scotland, where they provided most of the seasonal labour on Lowland farms. The Londonderry and Lough Swilly Railway track that moved west from Letterkenny as the L&BER (Letterkenny and Burtonport Extension Railway), that would run from Derry and terminate at Burtonport on the west coast, was only being laid in 1898. A station at Crolly, the eastern frontier of the Rosses, and another at Meenbanad, to the west, meant that the Rosses migrants — children and adults — on their way to farms in the Laggan or in Scotland wouldn't have to walk to Fintown, which was thirteen miles from Dungloe, the Rosses' only town. The L&BER track was completed and the railway opened in March 1903.

The town land of Meendernasloe lies a little to the east of the branch road that runs from the village of Annagry to Loughanure to the south. The area is still a *Gaeltacht* where the first language (and language of choice) is Irish. In 1898, due to its isolation, a long tradition of folk practice and social interaction was still more or less intact though peripherally aware of coming changes. Frank Sweeney, from Annagry, wrote an exemplary detailed sociological study of the area immediate to his birthplace using a local murder as its focus. Published in 2002, *The Murder of Conell Boyle, County Donegal, 1898* has become an essential text in the social history of the county. The seasonal migration had caused some alleviation in the labour that was necessary for survival but life was still hard. Children as young as eight had to leave home and family to work for often cruel and indifferent masters. It was received wisdom that you should hire yourself to a Protestant master because it was unlikely that you would have to work the Sabbath.

The houses were usually of one room with a turf-burning fire at one end and beds that doubled as settles during the day. Potatoes were still the staple diet, now more or less blight-proof thanks to copper sulphate, and with vegetable gardens, pocket-handkerchief-sized hay fields for cow fodder, and money earned from seasonal work to buy tea, flour and finance visits to pubs, pay church dues and pay rents, life was, if not comfortable, then providing 'a gait of going', according to another Rosses writer, Peadar O'Donnell. In such a community as Meendernasloe family connections were paramount and relationships with neighbours, often blood relatives, were significant. The Irish proverb, 'People live in each other's shadows' was applicable here. Life, however, was not all footing turf or moulding potatoes. There were sports and horse races as described in JM Synge's *The Playboy of the Western World*. Wakes had a long tradition of not very decorous games, frowned on by the Church but echoing an ancient, even pagan, asseveration of life against death. The dark evenings of winter were brightened by *oicheanta airneáil* (visiting nights) when neighbours gathered in a local house to beguile the time with music, song and storytelling about the ancient heroes of Ireland. One set of tales was known by the collective title of *Fiannaíocht*, and concerned Fionn Mac Cumhaill and the warriors of the *Fianna*. Even more popular were ghost stories which left nervous neighbours afraid to go home alone in the dark.

There were great celebrations when the 'tattie-howkers', or migrants, arrived home at the end of their stints. Alcohol was a serious past-time and potentially could lead to breakdown in communication. There were drunken quarrels, grudge fights, imagined slights reacted to and old scores settled, but wilful murder of one local by another was extremely rare. When one did happen ten years previously in neighbouring Gweedore, it caused a sensation but comment was internal and not for outside ears. In June 1888 Nancy Ferry, a woman of sixty-seven from the district of Lunniagh, north of Derrybeg, was attacked by Bella McIlwaine, a neighbour half her age. The victim was beaten about the head with a stone until believed dead and then her body was shoved into the hot embers of the fireplace. McIlwaine was arrested when Nancy died eight weeks later in August. In December she was tried for murder in Derry's courthouse in spite of claiming that the old woman had been drunk and fallen in the fire. No drink was found in Nancy's house and the medical evidence of attack by a heavy instrument was incontrovertible. The jury took an hour and a half to find her guilty and she was sentenced to be hanged on 4 January 1889 in Derry Jail. However, the *Derry Journal* reported that the hanging of a woman was causing a lot of discomfort and moves were afoot to have the capital sentence reduced to life imprisonment. An eleventh-hour reprieve was granted on the grounds that there was a long history of ill-feeling between the two women which had not been revealed during the trial.

There was general disbelief when the body of sixty-year-old Conell Boyle was discovered by his twelve-year-old grandniece, Ellen O'Donnell, just before 7am on the morning of Wednesday, 31 August 1898. Ellen, who often stayed with her grandmother, was sent to Boyle's house with milk and found him lying on his back. He lay near the fireplace, his head covered in blood and his hands cold and stiff. She raced back the short distance to her grandmother, Mary, the dead man's sister, who screamed and ran to check if he might still be alive. When she saw that there was nothing to be done, she sent Ellen to tell her father James and mother Nancy, Mary's daughter, to come. She was later sent the short distance to Annagry to inform the priest and the police. It was just after 9am that Acting-Sergeant McMacken was told of the fatality. He went at once with two constables to Boyle's house to meet if not actual hostility, then nearly impenetrable reserve. The RIC were regarded with suspicion as alien, English-speaking, entities that usually meant trouble. McMacken was probably tolerant of such attitudes in a philosophical kind of way, even if implied difficulties in the investigation.

There were bloodstains on Boyle's shirt and vest and also on the stones in the 'street', as the locals call the space in front of houses. The police found part of a blood-stained barrel stave that they suspected to be the murder weapon. Boyle's drawstring purse was missing and robbery was assumed to be the motive. As the *Derry Journal* of Friday, 5 September, rather graphically described it:

> ...his body was found lying in the kitchen, the head

> lacerated and covered with blood, and the pockets rifled.
> An inside vest, in which he was in the habit of carrying
> money, was turned inside out and full of blood.

It also reported that 'Mr Gaussen RM was early notified of the occurrence, and with County Inspector Dobbyns and District Inspector Bell, is vigorously engaged in carrying on an investigation with the intention, if possible, of discovering the murderer or murderers.' It also observed that the scene had been visited by large numbers; modern crime officers would be horrified at the thought of such wholesale contamination of the crime scene.

Among those suspected were a group of travelling tinsmiths who had camped by the side of the road that led from Annagry to Loughanure. They were questioned and later released. One gets the impression that the interrogation of the travellers was entirely procedural; experienced police officers naturally looked to members of the extended family. There was the curious incident of the dog in the night-time which hadn't barked at a possible intruder. The dog was loudly hostile to people it did not know, so the night visitor must have been familiar, a point carefully noted by the investigators.

Conell Boyle's two sons, Hugh and Charley, were working in Scotland that summer, Hugh in Peebles and Charley further south in Kelso. They had to be informed. Hugh's wife, Mary, should by custom have lived with Conell Boyle when Hugh was away but she and her father-in-law constantly quarrelled. She was young and full of new ideas and regularly left the Boyle household to go to her parents' home when there had been a disagreement. It was she who sent a telegram to her husband reading, 'Father found dead in the house this morning', but oddly she walked the five miles to the Gweedore hotel to dispatch the wire rather than use the post office in Annagry, hardly more than a mile from the house. Belief in the nosiness of post-mistresses was not uncommon and Sophie Duffy, the

Annagry official, was futher tainted by being a policeman's widow.

The post-mortem was carried out by Dr William Smyth, medical officer of Dungloe dispensary district, and his colleague, Dr Robert McLaughlin, at Boyle's house on the afternoon of Thursday, 1 September, while James Boyle from Stranorlar, the coroner for the district, presided at an inquest later that evening. Hugh Boner, Boyle's brother-in-law, was the first witness. He described how he found the body and concluded his evidence with a characteristic piece of local *béal druidte* (closed mouth): 'I heard of no dispute between the son and deceased. I know nothing more about the matter than what I have stated.' Cooperation with the law would continue to be minimal. The only surprise during the proceedings was Dr Smyth's stated opinion based on the depth of the mortal injuries that they could have been inflicted 'by a light weapon or a weapon used by a weak person. The wounds that caused death could not have been occasioned by a fall, nor could they have been self-inflicted. The arms and hands were uninjured, as if the deceased made no effort to defend himself.' The implication that a woman, perhaps the fiery Mary Boyle, the troublesome daughter-in-law, could have done it, was marked by the local people. He also said that the face of the deceased appeared to have been wiped clean, suggesting that someone with a sense of decency had tried to do a final right by Boyle. The inquest jury found 'that the deceased was murdered on the night of the 30th or morning of the 31st. By some person or persons unknown.'

Mary Boyle received a telegram from her husband the next day saying, 'Starting with boat tonight.' He would arrive sometime on the Saturday evening just in time for the funeral on the Sunday, 4 September. Due to the nature of the death the usual wake jollifications would not take place. Hugh reached Meendernasloe at 7.30 and by 11pm had been arrested by DI Bell for the murder of his father. Constable Dickson, in whose charge he was placed, cautioned him but his own underwear had already let him down. The *Derry Journal* of 5 October reports Hugh telling Dickson, 'I'm in a nice fix. It was the blood on my drawers that told all.' It became clear that Boyle left the bothy at Shipley Farm near Peebles at about 6pm on Monday 29 August, telling his mate, Mick O'Donnell, that he was going to see some sick friends in Edinburgh and would return on Thursday 1 September. At noon the next day he boarded the Glenties train at Strabane. The Burns-Laird steamer service between Derry quay and the Broomielaw in Glasgow was regular and efficient, even if the 'Scotch boats' were badly in need of stabilisers.

Boyle rather wisely engaged Ellen Mulherrin and Annie Smith in jokey conversation. They were two servant girls, on their way to service with a Captain Stewart who lived near Dungloe. It suggests that he had no thought of murder in his mind but simply wanted to settle matters with his abrasive father. Bernard Devine, an RIC constable, whose duty required him to be on the platform at Fintown to meet the Strabane train was able to place him there on Tuesday, 30 August. Bella McLoone, the wife of the owner of McLoone's pub, served him a drink at the same time. He hoped to get a lift with the girls en route to Dungloe but the driver of the car refused. He did get a lift a short while later with a man called Duffy who took him first to Doochary, four miles away, where they and the passengers in the other car stopped for another drink. William O'Donnell, the owner of the pub, was another who was later able to testify, if necessary, that he was there on Tuesday afternoon. Another witness was Brigid Magill, O'Donnell's maid, who gave him tea. He climbed the famous curly road out of Doochary and began the eight mile journey to Dungloe but was soon given a lift by Francis McGinley who took him as far as the 'Wee Bridge' in the town, arriving at 6pm. From there he made his way by back roads the six or seven miles to Meendernasloe.

This efficient tracking became clear at the trial, which was held at the Belfast winter assizes, beginning on Thusday, 8

December 1898. There were enough witnesses to cover his journey from Fintown to the Wee Bridge, though a kind of qualified *béal druidte* operated there too. Brigid Magill would not identify him with any certainty as the man to whom she served tea in Doochary, saying he was like the prisoner 'but she would not swear that it was really him', and Duffy was also not sure. As stated in the *Derry Journal* of 9 December, 'Whether it was from extreme caution or through some other feeling, Duffy would not identify the prisoner as being positively the man but he was ready to swear he was very like him.' After the Wee Bridge it was as if he were invisible. There were no witnesses who could be persuaded to testify that they had seen him. At the end of August it was bright till 9pm and, though the bog roads he travelled had few houses, Annagry was well-populated. Mouths were clamped tight; the community had its own way of dealing with malefactors.

The likely account of how he came to kill his father is contained in Hugh's 1909 petition for release. Three months after he arrived in Shipley he received a letter from his wife saying that her father-in-law had threatened to cut her head off if she tried to harvest the crops that Hugh had put in. He got a similar letter from his father, written probably by his niece because he was illiterate. Knowing the old man's fierce temper he left immediately for home but when he arrived, Conell ordered him to leave the house, 'rising the stick above me.' Hugh wrested the stick out of his hands but then his father rushed to a pile of stones. 'I saw if he got one my life would be in danger. I struck him a random blow and he fell upon the stones… it was all done upon the impulse of the moment. I took him up and brought him in.' If this is a true account of what happened the charge should not have been of murder — at most manslaughter, if not actual self-defence.

The Crown, led by John Atkinson QC MP, the Attorney-General for Ireland, insisted that his purpose in coming was with the deliberate intention of removing his irascible father,

CONELL BOYLE

with his endless disputes and jealous preservation of his own rights. As Atkinson put it, 'He might have supposed that if he got his father out of the way he would have securer hold upon the house and holding, besides terminating for ever the disputes about the stones [taken by him from his father to build his own house and not paid for] and about payment for the cropping.' What was most suspicious was his speedy return to Scotland. He walked the twenty miles from the house where his father lay dead and bought 'the only ticket issued that day to Londonderry'. He reached his bothy, as he promised his mate Mick O'Donnell, on 1 September, just in time to receive Mary's telegram about the death. His precipitate return was a clumsy attempt to establish an alibi and the combination of the telegram from his wife and his deliberately misleading answer looked like further conspiratorial bungling.

Hugh did not take the witness stand, which may have been a tactical error on the part of his defence. If he could have told his story as he did in his appeal statement the jury might have appreciated his situation a little better. Surprisingly he found an ally in the presiding judge, the Lord Chief Justice, Sir Peter O'Brien, then at the height of his reputation. He was a Catholic but not regarded as a friend of nationalist Ireland. He was known, especially in the Munster circuit, as 'Pether the Packer' because of frequent accusations of loading juries. At this trial held in Belfast, a mere 130 miles from Annagry but light years away in sympathy or understanding of the people and the society in which they lived, he was conscious that this jury would find it hard to empathise with either the witnesses or the accused. In his address to them he did all but put the word 'manslaughter' in their mouths but the jurors did not perform as he wished. They returned a verdict of wilful murder but asked for clemency on account of his youth — he was twenty-two. O'Brien had no choice then but to impose the death penalty:

> The sentence of the court is that I do hereby adjudge and

> order that you, Hugh Boyle, be taken… to Her Majesty's prison in the county of Derry and that you be kept there until Thursday the 12th day of January, which shall be the year of our Lord, 1899. And that you be taken to the common place of execution within the walls of the said prison in which you shall be then confined and that you be then and there hanged by the neck until you are dead, and that your body be buried within the precincts of the prison… and may the Lord have mercy on your soul.

When he heard the verdict Boyle reeled backwards and, all the way to Derry Jail, 'wept bitterly almost the whole journey'.

The *Derry Journal*'s account of the last day of the trial concluded with the following paragraph:

> At a late hour last evening we learned on excellent authority that the death sentence passed upon Hugh Boyle on Saturday at the Ulster Winter Assizes will probably be commuted by his Excellency the Lord Lieutenant, and therefore there is every likelihood that the extreme penalty of the law will not be carried into effect.

Pleas for mitigation to Lord Cadogan were sent by James Boyle, the coroner of West Donegal, by Pether the Packer himself, and priests from the Rosses. Cadogan commuted the sentence to penal servitude for life on 22 December and a relieved Boyle was transferred from Derry to prison in Port Laoise, known then as Maryborough after Queen Mary Tudor. He served ten years until his release after several petitions by himself and his wife who, perhaps wisely, had left the Rosses and gone to live in Bayonne, New Jersey. On 7 September 1909 he left Maryborough and immediately crossed the Atlantic to Bayonne to join her. They ran a boarding-house together in which many of their clients were from Donegal, and Hugh never returned to Ireland. He died sometime in the 1940s, survived by the fiery Mary for another twenty years. Unquestionably he did kill his father but it clearly was not his intention. His death sentence demonstrated a lack of empathy by all his legal adversaries, except for O'Brien, who showed mercy.

8
JOHN FLANAGAN

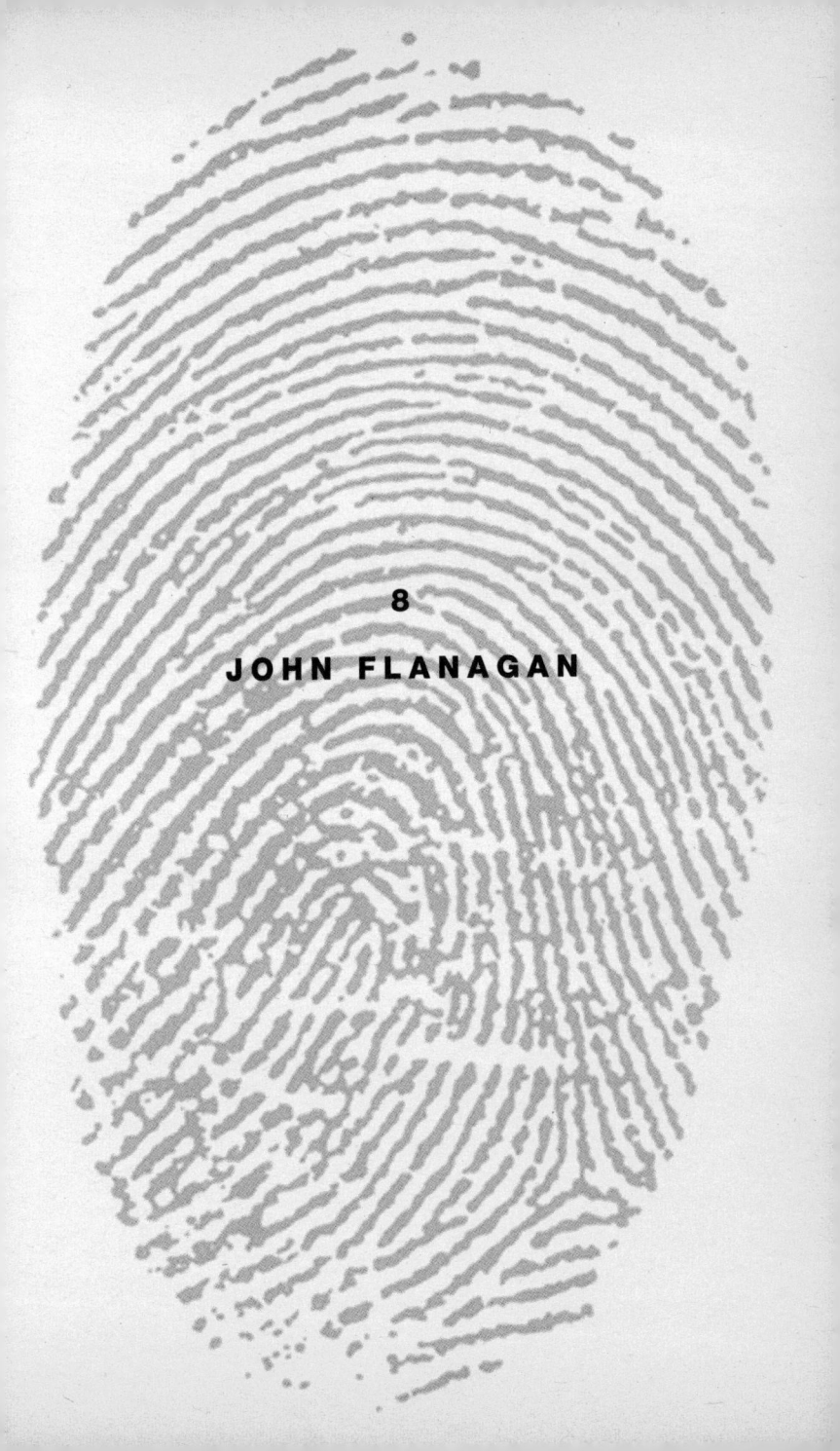

THE TOWN OF CLONES is officially in County Monaghan but so close to the border with Fermanagh as to underline the artificiality of the county boundaries established when the shiring of Ireland took place at the start of the seventeenth century. In 1903 such divisions had little impact on the lives of the people. Clones, though small, was an important market town and on market days its clients came from Fermanagh, Tyrone and Cavan as well as Monaghan. It had several small private slaughterhouses, including the one that was run by the Fee family at their property in Jubilee Road. An inevitable result of a private slaughterhouse is that offal, the unusable parts of the animal carcase, tends to accumulate and incessantly makes its presence felt. The Fee brothers, Joseph and George, also had a vegetable garden and the animal manure proved useful as fertiliser. The trouble was that the combination of dead offal and manure was hugely offensive. Apart from olfactory sensitivity a loaded dung-heap was a serious health hazard, especially since it lay in open ground beside the Fee house.

Eventually, the townspeople's complaints got louder and Terence O'Neill, the town sergeant (an archaic term for a council official, sometimes called 'town surveyor'), with council authority, ordered the Fees to get rid of the nuisance. On 15 December 1903, on Joe Fee's instruction, Albert McCoy, helped by the young John Farmer, arrived with a cart and began the unpleasant job of dismantling the large heap of dirt. The wage for the work was the use of the manure and McCoy readily understood when Fee told him to leave some manure for use in his cabbage patch. When the heap had been greatly diminished after five cartloads had been taken away McCoy reminded Farmer to leave some against the Fee's fence. As he continued to scrape away, his fork hit against a boot buried in the dung. He tried to spear it on the prong of his pitchfork but it would not yield. To his horror he realised why — there was a foot in it. In fact it was part of a body that had been buried under the manure and offal for some time.

Later examination showed that the grave was six feet long and three feet wide but unfortunately for the murderer only two feet deep. McCoy rushed to the local RIC barracks to report his find and Head Constable McKeown hastened to the scene. After briefly examining the site he made his way to the Fee house in Jubilee Road, certain that the body was that of John Flanagan, who had gone missing almost exactly eight months earlier on 16 April.

On that market day Flanagan had had business with Joe Fee and there was a *prima facie* case that linked him to Flanagan's subsequent disappearance. This haste was procedurally inappropriate and the leader for the defence, the flamboyant George Hill Smith, at each of Joe Fee's three trials for murder made a lot of the rush to judgement by McKeown before the body had been exhumed. In spite of its having been heavily sprinkled with quicklime, Flanagan's cadaver was surprisingly well preserved. The dampness of the soil had acted as a slaking agent causing the corpse to be encrusted but not destroyed. Dr Tierney, who conducted the autopsy, said, as reported by the *Belfast News Letter*:

> ...the body was in a soapy state and must have lain in the grave for at least six months. Between the coat and the waistcoat there was a casing of lime, the inside of the sleeve was also covered with lime... The body was lying on the right shoulder, partly on the face, with the legs from the knees downwards protruding upwards at right angles

to the body. In the case of death from sudden violence rigor mortis was generally well marked in six hours.

A number of witnesses helped with the final identification and later corroborated their statements at the Belfast hearing. Patrick Clark said that he had sent the purse found in the pocket of the corpse to James Armstrong for mending and Armstrong confirmed that the stitching was his. Edward Carey said that he had made the boots that started the whole investigation and Terence McIlroy, a local tailor, 'identified the trousers as having been made by him for Flanagan'. The state of the body was such that identification was possible only by means of the boots, clothing and false teeth. (The statement made in court by the Solicitor-General, JH Campbell KC MP, gives a stark insight into the social history of the period in that the fact that a twenty-one-year-old with false teeth caused no comment.) Death, according to Tierney, was caused by trauma to the base of the skull, showing a hole five-eighths by four-eighths of an inch caused by a homemade weapon with a spike at each end. There was also a perpendicular cut in the throat that sliced through the Adam's apple, which was probably caused by the pig-sticking knife that had tumbled out of the clothing of the corpse when it was exhumed.

The technique was once associated with animal slaughter in which the knife was inserted into the carcase above the breastbone and wrenched upwards into the throat. The knife was sent to Richard Jackson Moss, chemical analyst to the Royal Dublin Society. It was encrusted with clay and lime and when the analyst removed the wooden handle he found portions of pig's bristle. Very recently a method for differentiating between mammalian and animal had been devised and Moss was able to prove that though there were stains of animal blood on the trousers one large stain on the inside leg was definitely human.

As we have seen McKeown felt that he knew already who had killed Flanagan. His progress with Sergeant Young down

Fermanagh Street towards the Fee house in Jubilee Road at 7pm on a December evening was quickly noted in the small town that was still bewildered by the disappearance of the well-known egg middleman. One of Fee's casual helpers, Edward Howard, was standing at Nicholl's Corner, watching the posse heading towards the Fee house. Joe Fee came over and asked him what all the fuss was about. He told Howard to go and see but his young neighbour refused, fearing 'there might be a row'. Fee started off for his house and was found there by McKeown, looking very pale, embracing his bewildered mother and sister. The mother kept asking what was wrong but Fee wouldn't say. He left with the head constable after being arrested for 'wilfully murdering John Flanagan'.

From evidence gathered in Fee's three trials, an account of the day of the murder was formed. The market day fell on Thursday, 16 April 1903. It was an important event in the commercial life of the town. John Flanagan, acting for his father, was what was known as a 'higgler', travelling around farms buying up eggs and selling them at a profit. The Flanagan family never missed a fair day in Clones and farmers from all around brought the freshly laid eggs to their stall. Before 1.30pm a large amount of eggs were already boxed and ready to go to Belfast by the up-train on the GNR. John Flanagan was in charge of the stall that day and had been given a float of £30 in cash and two cheques — one for £50 and another for £5 — which he would cash at the Ulster Bank. These were considerable sums of money, totalling perhaps £8,000 in today's currency. The pitch was set up in the Diamond, right in the centre of town, and it was there that Joseph Connolly and Patrick Moan, his usual helpers, joined Flanagan who had driven into town with his pony and trap.

After about an hour's busy dealing Flanagan decided he needed more ready cash and went off to the Ulster Bank to cash his cheques. He was paid in single pound notes, which he put in his pockets. On the way to the bank he met Joe Fee who owed him £2. Fee asked Flanagan to accompany him to his house so he could pay him immediately. However, it was a busy time of day and Flanagan was reluctant to leave the stall. He told Fee he would see him later instead but Fee insisted that he come to the house about 11am. He said he wanted to buy Flanagan a drink at Creighton Duggan's public house once he paid him back. Flanagan agreed but when he turned up at the Fee house there was no sign of Fee. He waited impatiently for nearly an hour and then returned to the Diamond to help with the crating of eggs for the train. His two assistants teased him about timekeeping and complained that they had been run off their feet. They noticed that sometime after noon their boss pulled a wad of notes out of his pocket to pay Patrick McDermott a bill for egg-boxes. At about 12.30pm Flanagan was tapped on the shoulder and turned to find Fee asking what happened to him: 'What took you away? What hurry were you in?' Flanagan replied, 'I waited long enough and I had my stuff to send out for the train.'

Fee persuaded him to come with him: 'Come down. I've got that for you now.' In his testimony at the Belfast trial, Patrick Moan described how Flanagan glanced at him and Moan had joked in reply, 'Be another hour away this time?' Flanagan slapped him on the back and said, 'Hurry, Pat. I'll be back in ten minutes.' His anxiety to go with Fee was based on the latter's notorious reluctance in paying debts. That was the last time that Moan saw him. He was seen briefly about 1pm on Jubilee Road opposite the slaughterhouse by a Peter Owens and no more after that. In his eagerness to have the debt paid he did not think to insist that Fee bring the money to the pitch. Moan and Connolly continued to work, reassuring the farmers that John would come and pay them for their eggs. Their anxiety grew as the time of the train's departure approached and the crowds of people waiting to be paid grew vociferous. Flanagan was missing and so was Fee. He did not reappear until 3pm, not having been seen for the two hours after leaving the Flanagan pitch, except briefly when he ran into James Nicholl's store, picked up a spade and cried, 'Put this down to me', and ran out again.

Moan and Connolly did their best to reassure the impatient people waiting for their money and decided to send for the father. They got their eggs safely on the train and sent word to the Flanagan household that John had gone missing. Annie Flanagan hurried into town and began to look for her brother while her father placated the farmers and paid them their money. At about 3pm she reached the Fee house. Mrs Fee answered the door but had no information about her brother, saying that she hadn't seen him since Christmas. Annie returned to the egg stand and found Fee there. She asked him if he had seen John and Fee said that he had met him in Creighton Duggan's and paid him the £2 that he owed him. She wanted to know if they had been drinking but he reassured her that they had only two half-glasses of wine. Fee volunteered to accompany her in the search and they went first to Duggan's where he offered to buy her a drink but she refused. They next went to the Hibernian Hotel but John had not been seen there either. Fee suggested that Annie return to the stand but she preferred to keep looking. She was walking a little ahead of Fee and when she turned to speak she found that he was gone. When next they met he reassured her, saying, 'John will turn up. He's in town.'

The fair was over by evening. The dealers had closed up their stands and the farmers had all gone home. The disappearance was reported to the police but their enquiries came to nothing. John Flanagan was missing without trace. Fee had been seen with him enough times during the day to fall under suspicion but when asked his usual reply was: 'Oh, it'll be all right. He's gone off with some woman or other.' Fee preserved a remarkable coolness throughout. His offer to accompany Annie Flanagan was to ensure that she went nowhere near the slaughterhouse. There was a circus in town that night and Fee was in the crowd apparently enjoying the show. His financial situation seemed to have greatly improved. Before this he had shown signs of hardship. On 9 April he bought nine pigs from a Mr May and sold them a short while later, making very little on the deal. He had initially asked May for some time to pay but when May called at the Fee house, a week after Flanagan's disappearance, Fee paid him the £6 he was owed in single notes. The day after the fair he went to Ballybay, which was twenty-five miles away, and paid £25 in notes for pigs. His slaughterhouse was low-grade; the animals he slaughtered were far from their prime. He handled mostly 'cases', old and ailing animals that could not be sold on the open market. Yet on the day after his visit to Ballybay he paid £18 to a farmer named Dawson for a 'fine fat beast'. It was also noticed that he had enclosed his dung heap with a close-set fence replacing the open fence that had previously been there.

Flanagan's 'soapy' and encrusted body was taken to Cassidy's public house, because it was the nearest licensed premises to the scene. Cassidy objected but the coroner advised him that he had no alternative in law. The actual inquest was held in Creighton Duggan's pub and when all the evidence was heard the jury found that Fee had killed Flanagan — their verdict was not unexpected but they could only advise. The prisoner had to be tried in an assize court. He appeared at the Monaghan spring assizes and again at the summer assizes. In each case the jury disagreed. In the first trial eight jurors found Fee guilty and four dissented; in the second trial only one dissented — at that time legal practice required total agreement, hence the question put to the foreman of any jury: 'Is that the verdict of you all?' In case of local prejudice or favour the third trial was held in Belfast, in the Crumlin Road courthouse. It began on Thursday, 1 December 1904, almost a year after the grisly find in Jubilee Road. Fee had spent the time in Armagh Jail with two excursions to court in Monaghan.

There was a certain amount of difficulty about swearing in the jury. As the *Irish News and Belfast Morning News* (the forerunner of today's *Irish News*) of 2 December reported, 'There were nineteen challenges by the defence', and several members of the jury panel excused themselves because of having already made up their minds about the case; one had a conscientious objection to capital punishment. The judge, Mr Justice Wright, challenged him that this was an objection to the laws of the country but the man replied, 'No, my lord, but I object to capital punishment.' James H Campbell, the Solicitor-General, leading for the prosecution, said he might be excused. The judge sternly remarked, 'The Crown seems to have an objection to your serving', and the abolitionist pertly replied, 'I am much obliged to the Crown', causing one of the few lighter moments in the case. Two other jurors excused themselves on the same grounds of conscience. The showy George Hill Smith, who had put up a bravura defence at the earlier hearings, seemed reluctant to lead in this case. There was some problem about the fees for his last two appearances. He was chided by both the judge and the Solicitor-General for mentioning fees at this juncture and with reluctance and as 'a man of honour' said, 'I have no intention of deserting this man and his family in their hour of need.' And so the trial began.

The Solicitor-General stated that,

> ...it was well for both the prisoner and the Crown that the case should be tried in an impartial venue, where there would be neither fear, favour or affection. Let them not be deterred that this was the third time of trial.

The prosecution evidence was pretty damning; Fee's disappearance at the same time and for the same period as Flanagan's, the obvious improvement in his financial situation, the surrounding of his midden by a closed fence, the discovery of Flanagan's body in the midden, and lastly, but by no means least, the fact that Flanagan's purse was found in his possession. After his initial reluctance, George Hill Smith swung into dramatic action for the defence. He was essentially a performer, the silk as actor, and with a fine array of words he did not disappoint his audience. It was a limited audience because the court authorities had permitted entrance only to those materially connected with the case. However, as the *News Letter* noted, 'Outside in the quadrangle hundreds of people had collected, and the passages were almost blocked up owing to the throng.' It was a case described by the *Irish News and Belfast Morning News* as 'the sensational Clones murder — a tragedy that for cowardice and brutality stands unparalleled in the history of crime in this country'. The proprietors of the *Belfast Evening Telegraph* were clearly delighted with 'one of the most sensational and extraordinary murder trials that have been known in the annals of crime in Ireland' because their reporters stated on Friday, 2 December, that: 'Last night's edition of the *Evening Telegraph* was bought up like wildfire, and the printing machines had to be kept going to a late hour to supply the town and country requirements.'

Smith's defence repeated the same points he had made at the other trials. He reminded the jurors that they should banish all preconceptions from their minds about the charge and about the accused. According to the *News Letter* report, 'He asked them, he beseeched them, he implored them, as far as human mind could do it, to divest themselves of all previously conceived prejudices.' There was much more in this vein but substantially his defence was that all the Crown's evidence was circumstantial. He criticised Head Constable McKeown for arresting Fee before the body was even recovered from the ground. As the *Irish News and Belfast Morning News* reported in Saturday's paper:

> It was that that set the bells a-ringing and from that hour to the present the prisoner had been hounded down in the public prints, condemned the moment of his arrest without a particle of evidence. The head constable had his suspicions. Counsel would not have complained if he had arrested Fee on suspicion but what he did complain of was

that without any knowledge whatever, he should
anticipate the disinterers and resurrectionists and assume
that the body was that of Flanagan.

He asked them to look at Fee and consider if he presented the appearance of a man callous in character. Rather he was a man pilloried by 'the underlings of the Press who were glad to get hold of any scrap of information and to ring it round with feathers of their own invention.' Though eloquent, Smith's long defence and generally unreliable witnesses failed to convince the jury. Two of his witnesses could not attend the court on Friday, 2 December, because in Smith's words, 'They had been dining too well,' to which Mr Justice Wright replied, 'You mean they have been drinking.' Smith said that was so.

Saturday, 3 December was the final day of the trial. The early part consisted mainly of evidence by defence witnesses trying unsuccessfully to give sightings of Fee in the period between 12.30 and 3.30pm. Admission to the court was limited still, as the *News Letter* of the following Monday reported:

> Hundreds had early gathered in the hope of obtaining entrance, but a strong force of police under District-Inspector Clayton, kept the passages and quadrangle clear, and only jurors, witnesses, and others having business were allowed to pass the barrier. Non-admittance, however, was not sufficient to drive the people away. They loitered quietly outside in the open square, and testified their absorbing interest by remaining the entire day, questioning every passer-out as to the progress of the case.

The report praised the speech for the defence of 'the old man eloquent of the North-East circuit' but remarked that 'no counsel, however ingenious, can overthrow hard facts with a wave of the hand or a rhetorical outburst'. The judge's summing-up for the jury lasted three and a half hours, as he patiently and painstakingly went through the events of 16 April

1903, interpreting the significance of every piece of evidence.

The jury were dismissed to consider their verdict at 5.25pm. They returned one hour later with a guilty verdict. Fee, who remained impassive throughout his trials, showed no emotion when the verdict was announced. When asked by the judge if he had anything to say, he replied, 'Well, My lord, the evidence sworn against me was all lies. I swear I am innocent. I am not afraid.' Wright placed the black silk square on his judicial wig and pronounced the death sentence; Fee was to be executed on 22 December 1904 in Armagh Jail. His closing remarks were reported in all the papers:

> A jury of the citizens of Belfast, apart from the county where you carry on your trade, were irresistibly impelled by the overwhelming weight of evidence against you that yours was the hand that struck down John Flanagan. No honest juror could have come to any other conclusion. The crime you committed was of a singularly cold-blooded and treacherous nature and was impelled by one base and sordid motive — love of money and your lust for money. I only wish to warn you against cherishing any hope of mercy in this world and I would entreat you, in the short time at your disposal, to prepare to meet your doom and make your peace with God and pray for pardon and forgiveness for your sins.

By direction of his Lordship, the jurors who tried the case were excused from further attendance at the assizes.

The executioner was Henry Pierrepoint, one of three members of the same family who acted in the official capacity for the Home Office. He had been appointed in 1901 after considerable lobbying of the officials in charge of capital punishment. During his nine years of office he carried out 105 hangings. He lost his post in 1910 when he turned up for an execution 'considerably the worse for drink' at Chelmsford prison in Essex. His elder brother Thomas succeeded him and was later replaced by

Henry's son, Albert, in 1946. They took their role seriously and skilfully ensured that death, resulting from a broken neck due to the position of the large knot, was mercifully quick. To prevent crowds gathering at Armagh Jail, especially on Barrack Hill, which overlooked the jail yard, 'the authorities had taken steps to ensure the utmost privacy'. The *Irish News* further reported that a large canvas sheet prevented a view of the passage-way from the condemned cell to the scaffold. 'The sides of the scaffold were, however, plainly visible.'

The prisoner attended Mass and received communion but took nothing else to eat or drink that morning, three days before Christmas. The prison chaplain, Father Sheerin, and Father Gavin accompanied him to the platform, reciting the litany for the dying. Henry Pierrepoint placed a white cap over Fee's head so that he wouldn't see the execution platform. He was led to the trapdoor with pinioned arms and there had his legs strapped together. The rope, in which silk threads were mixed in with the hemp to prevent slipping, was placed around his neck with the eyelet fixed under the left ear so that the drop would cause the spinal cord to be broken. At 8am Henry pulled the lever and Fee's body crashed down. At the statutory inquest Dr JM Palmer, the prison surgeon, confirmed that death was due to strangulation. Asked by John A Peel, the coroner, if he thought that it was instantaneous, Palmer said yes, 'and in my judgement was carried out quickly and expeditiously'. The coroner's jury returned the following verdict:

> ...the said Joseph Fee, being at the time of his death a male prisoner of the age of twenty-two years, was a prisoner in His Majesty's prison at Armagh, under the sentence of death for the murder of one John Flanagan, and the judgement of death was duly executed on him by his being hanged by the neck until dead within the walls of said prison on the date and year aforesaid, and not twenty-four hours before the holding of this inquest, and that the body

> on which this inquest is held is the identical body of the said Joseph Fee as aforesaid.

So ended the story and the life of young Joe Fee and with him the answers to many questions: When exactly did he decide to kill Flanagan? Was it when he realised that Flanagan had quite a lot of money — money he sorely needed? What was he doing when he was meant to be meeting Fee at 11am that morning? As with so much else the full truth will never be known.

9
WILLIAM BARBER

SOME YEARS AGO, when mature unmarried ladies in Derry were good-humouredly teased about their lack of husbands a common riposte was, 'Sure maybe I'll get an oul' policeman!' Fanny Malone, a native of that city, did just that. In August 1912 she married William Barber; he had been a sergeant in the Royal Irish Constabulary but had retired in 1909 when he was transferred to Belfast. Fanny was in her mid-thirties and William was fifty-six, a considerable gap, though less commented upon then than it might be now. He was also considerably taller than his wife as he was well over six feet in height while she was well under five feet. They lived in Belfast until 1921 when he sold his house and bought two adjacent houses in Cultra, on the Belfast Lough, as the Irish name ('back of the strand') implies. Barber was a widower with two adult children; his son was in the merchant navy and his daughter was a nurse. Since his first wife's death in 1907 his niece, Isobel Frances Martin, had been his housekeeper and she stayed on after his marriage.

Officers of the RIC were, with rare exceptions, highly respectable and prudent with money. They had a steady wage and a sound pension, and they were encouraged to be disciplined in their financial matters. In Barber's case the habit of frugality persisted at the time of his death, twenty-two years after leaving the force. He found a job as a rent collector for the firm of A&J Turner, who owned a lot of slum properties. Barber retained his revolver from his service days and was accustomed to carry it loaded in his pocket for his protection, not so much through fear of robbery but rather because he feared violence during the actual collection. The revolver was kept on top of the wardrobe when not in use.

Barber was seventy-eight and still in excellent health by the Christmas of 1933. His carefulness with money had resulted in a reputation for miserliness. In her statement to Constable Kierin, Fanny called him a 'scringe' but like many other of her remarks to the interviewing officers she later denied having made it. She had said, 'He was an old scringe. He never gave me anything, only what barely kept the house.' At Cultra the Barbers shared the larger of the two houses with Isobel Martin; the other was demolished and a bungalow was built on the site. At the time of the murder it was occupied by a tenant, Peter Conlan. In October 1933 he complimented Fanny about the vigour and good health of her elderly husband and she had replied, 'I wonder if the old fool will never die.' As Conlan observed at the Derry trial, 'I took it as a joke.' At 8.30pm on Christmas Eve, Conlan heard two unusual noises; he described the first as sounding like a picture falling from a wall and the second, about twenty minutes later, like a car door being slammed. The walls of the bungalow were quite thin and Conlan often heard ordinary noises from the Barber house.

He was startled some time later by a vigorous knocking at his backdoor and found Isobel Martin and Fanny Barber standing there, both looking tense and excited. Fanny asked him to come over to her house immediately because, 'Something's happened.' Isobel added, 'Auntie's in terrible trouble.' It was a pretty damning thing to say, suggesting as it did that Auntie had done something she shouldn't. Fanny asked the puzzled Conlan if he had seen a prowler in her garden and he said no but he did describe the strange sounds he had heard. He followed the two women round to the back of the house, through the garage. He asked what was wrong with the front door and Fanny answered, 'My darling's lying in the hall.' When she opened the back door the Barbers' two dogs ran up barking as they did when any stranger approached the house.

WILLIAM BARBER

William Barber lay against the locked front door. He had a gunshot wound behind his right ear and another in his chest. Isobel screamed and fainted at the sight, caught by Conlan before she hit the floor. He ran back to the bungalow to phone the police and then returned to check if William was definitely dead. Sergeant Patton and Constables Emo and Keirin arrived from Holywood Barracks, about a mile and a half away, accompanied by Dr Lawrence Donnan, who pronounced Barber dead. The entry behind the ear was blackened with gunpowder residue showing the bullet had been fired at very close range. Both entry wounds showed a downward trajectory. The revolver was a five-shooter and the chamber showed that three bullets had been fired and two remained in the gun. The third bullet could not then be found but was later discovered under a couch in the kitchenette having ricocheted from the chair in which it was presumed Barber was sitting when he was shot. (It was unearthed during a more thorough examination of the scene by District Inspector Lewis and County Inspector Regan on Christmas Day.) An examination of the body revealed that he still had his gold watch and chain and had in his pockets the substantial sum of £46, the equivalent of twenty weeks pay for a working man.

This seemed to rule out robbery as a motive for the attack and cast some doubt upon Fanny's story about a 'rough man who had been lurking in the garden'. About 8.30pm on Christmas Eve Fanny and William moved into the kitchenette so that he could listen to a religious programme on the wireless. It was presumably a battery set, which gave a clear reception unaffected by 'atmospherics', since Fanny said at her Derry trial that she lifted the family Bible and walked into the kitchenette and lit the gas. Her husband joined her and 'was just in the act of sitting down when this man rushed in'. According to her statement, she screamed and ran upstairs to her bedroom. She pushed over the bolt on her door and heard the gun shots. Her description of the intruder was not very precise; the man was in his forties with a red moustache and was wearing a dirty grey suit. His cap was pulled down to hide his face and he had a brown scarf round his neck.

The Barbers were alone in the house because Isobel Martin had gone with 'a visitor', Mrs Dornan, who had eaten her evening meal with the Barbers and now was returning to Dundonald to spend Christmas with her family. She was described as a visitor at the Derry trial but this may have been a piece of excessive respectability; she was almost certainly a lodger or why else should she have eaten with the Barbers before deciding to spend Christmas at her home? Barber had offered to accompany her as far as the Bangor Road where she would catch her bus into the city but Fanny would not hear of it. He was recovering from a cold, she insisted, and sent his niece in his place. Isobel was gone for over a half an hour and when she returned the front door was locked and she had to ring the bell. There was no response so she rang the bell again, prolonging the pressure. It was this loud ringing that brought Fanny round. She said at the Derry trial that when she recovered consciousness she was lying under the window. She looked out and told Isobel to come round to the back door. Her statement in the witness box was rather vague as to the detail of what she said to the niece, reflecting, no doubt, her extremely agitated mental state. She claimed she said, 'Isobel, darling, there has been a man come in and I heard something in the hall.' In floods of tears she ran down the stairs and out through the garage and round the side of the house to meet Isobel who took her by the arm as they entered again by the back door.

She said in court that she must have had a flash lamp (a battery torch) for when she saw 'the appearance of her own dear husband' she wanted to rush and pull him but Isobel prevailed. 'She pulled me away and we ran up to Mr Conlan's.' She continued to show extreme agitation and on St Stephen's Day her own doctor, Shane Magowan, examined her and had her admitted to Downpatrick mental hospital. She stayed there until the middle of May 1934, when she spent some time in a private nursing home in Knock, Belfast. There she was declared sane but advised to stay 'until her nerves got a little better'. It was there that she was arrested on 27 September and transferred to Armagh Jail. At the preliminary hearing in Holywood, Richard Carson, KC for the Crown, dismissed her story of the intruder and elicited from Isobel the mildly suspicious information that she had insurance policies taken out on her husband's life, a common enough practice. It was the inconsistencies in her statements made to Constables Emo and Keirin, most of which she denied in court in Derry, that alerted the police. The way that she directed Isobel and later Conlan away from the front door suggested that she knew her husband's body was propped against it. Then there was the fact that the two pet dogs had made no sound. It was enough to convince the Holywood magistrate who arranged for the trial to take place in Fanny's native city.

The trial opened in Derry on 7 December 1934 to considerable interest, though it was almost overshadowed by another case in which a Strabane man called McKenna was found guilty but insane in his wife's murder. Mr Justice Brown, the presiding judge, was famous in the city for his great size. In order to cater for his extra proportions an especially large bath had to be incorporated into the judicial lodgings in Carlisle Terrace. The Attorney-General, the Right Hon AB Babington KC MP, led for the Crown. He outlined his version of the events of 24 December 1933, stating that Barber had been shot between 8.30 and 8.40pm on Christmas Eve but ruled out suicide because of the position of the wounds and the angle of entry. He argued that the 'rough looking man' was an invention of the accused and that the door must have been locked before the killing since the body had been lying against it. The prosecution team called J Morris McKee, Fanny's solicitor, as a witness and required him to make public the terms of Barber's will — William had left everything to 'my dear wife'. McKee also disclosed that the insurance policies, which were taken by the Crown to be a further element of a possible motive, came to £272.

The defence led by William Lowry KC were able to produce a witness who said that a stranger had been in the district. A Mrs Elizabeth Richardson of Clanbrassil Terrace, Marino, a seafront district of Holywood, stated that at about 8.30 or 8.45pm on 24 December 1933 a man had called to her door and 'mentioned the name of Barber'. She told him there were people of that name living near Cultra. It was a muted, unsatisfactory piece of evidence and Lowry did not pursue it. Fanny had hoped to establish that, because of her husband's earlier profession and his present employment, his life was at risk. Lowry wondered if some old enemy might have followed him from Belfast but this suggestion made little impact. When he produced Barber's revolver, which, incidentally, had not yielded any fingerprints, Judge Brown cautioned Lowry to make sure that it was empty, remarking to some laughter, 'We don't want an accident happening here.' Lowry, with mannered counsel respect to the presiding judge, said, 'I'm glad your Lordship reminded me. I once saw an accident very nearly happening.' He held up the empty revolver and asked Fanny if she recognised it when it was shown to her at Conlan's house. She replied, 'Not at first.' Lowry then asked if her husband had a revolver. When she answered yes, he asked, 'What did your husband use it for?' She answered, 'For collecting rents, especially in the winter time.'

The Derry proceedings ended on Saturday, 8 December, with Mr Justice Brown's charge to the jury. He began by stating the legal principle that it was more important that they acquit the accused if in their opinion the Crown had not proved her guilty, than the murderer of William Barber being brought to justice. He took exception to the defence's criticism of the local police officers. As the *Derry Journal* reported, he said that it seemed to him that they had done their duty as well as they could. 'They had given their evidence very fairly and with every effort to bring out the truth as they knew it.' He commented on the absence of any sign of a struggle. He asked the jury to consider what the motive for the supposed assailant might have been, hardly robbery since the victim's gold watch and cash were still on his person. His address lasted about an hour and the jury were then sent away to consider his words as they sought a unanimous verdict. They were out for an hour and a half but could not agree. The judge accepted that they had made an honest effort and decided that there would no point in sending them back. With the agreement of counsel from both sides he adjourned the case for retrial to the spring assizes in County Down. The jury were excused service for the remainder of the current assizes.

The retrial was held in Downpatrick, on 10 March 1935, during a week of unseasonably icy and snowy weather, before the Lord Chief Justice Sir James Andrews, with the same counsel. No new evidence was offered and the trial consisted of claim and counterclaim by the same prosecution and defence teams. There was a suggestion that Fanny might offer a plea of 'guilty but of unsound mind', but she refused to do this. She might be saved from the hangman but would be penniless since she could not inherit if she was deemed insane, and the prospect of permanent confinement in a mental institution was hardly enticing. Babington again concentrated on the inconsistencies of her statements, the behaviour of the dogs and the length of her period of unconsciousness. Lowry, sensing that she was an unconvincing witness, concentrated on the lack of forensic evidence linking her with the shooting and suggested that it would be nearly impossible for a woman of her height to fire the bullets with a downward trajectory. The jury couldn't but appreciate that this argument had little value if, as it was demonstrated, Barber was seated at the time.

The jury had no doubt though they recommended mercy. Before the foreman could pronounce the guilty verdict Fanny screamed and fainted. Isobel also screamed and had to be led from the court. The *Londonderry Sentinel* described how 'a doctor hurriedly enter the dock; morphia was administered but Mrs Barber's shrieks rang through the court'. When Fanny had recovered it was to hear Lord Justice Andrews sentence her to be hanged by the neck until dead. The day of her execution was fixed for 5 April. Eventually, the death sentence was commuted to life imprisonment, partly due to the jury's recommendation. Fanny died seventeen years later in Armagh Jail.

Like most domestic tragedies the episode now seems pitiful rather than wicked. Women in general are less murderous that men and one can only guess at the tensions that caused the lethal use of the 'oul' policeman's gun. One wonders, too, about Isobel Martin's part, if any, in the story. Was there collusion? Did Isobel as housekeeper suffer from her uncle's meanness in the same way as his wife? Certainly she seemed to take Fanny's side in the affair and suffer great distress at her 'Guilty' verdict. Once again, we'll never know.

10

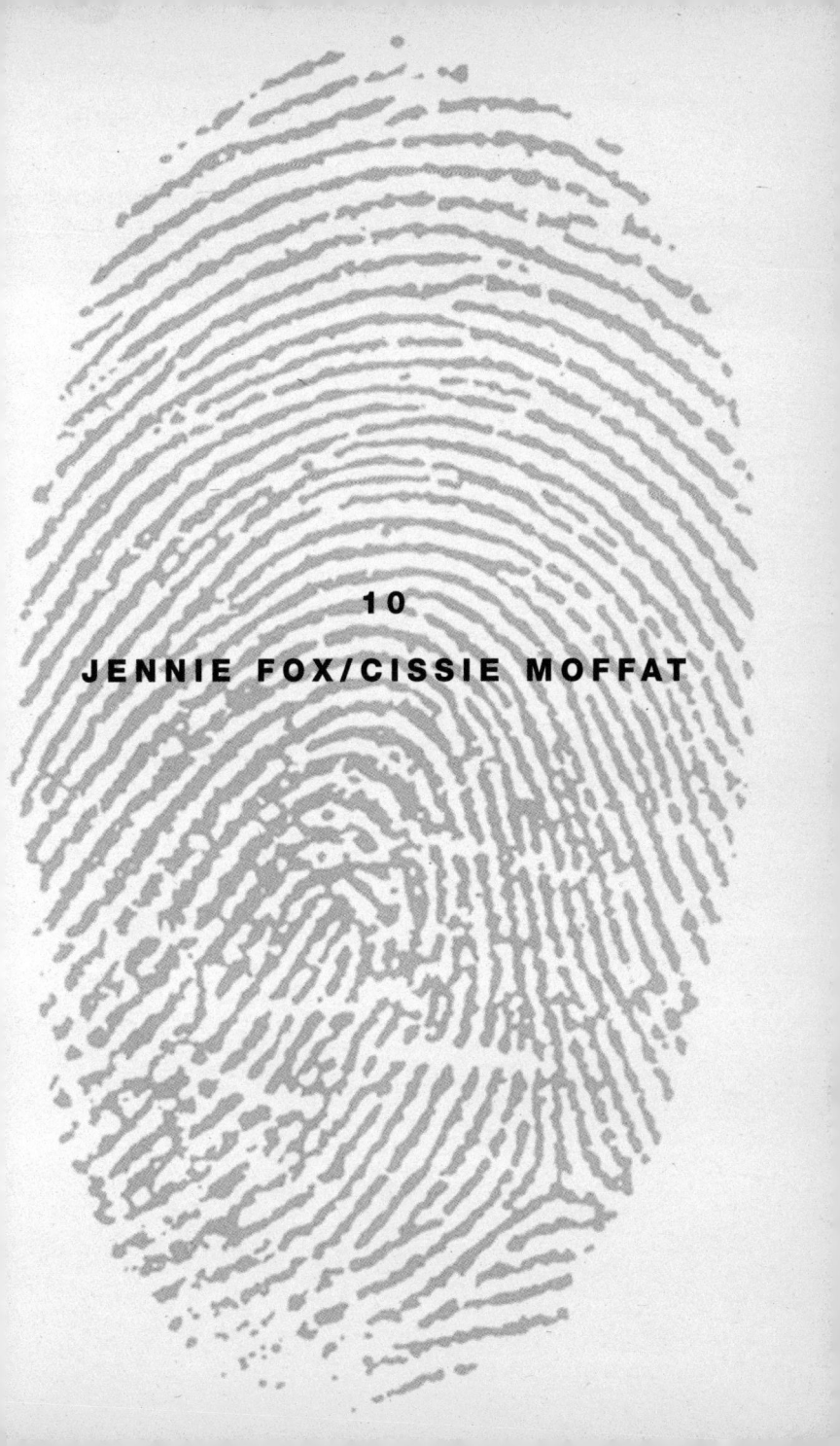

JENNIE FOX/CISSIE MOFFAT

ON MONDAY 18 JULY 1938 I stood with my two aunts at the top of Great James's Street in Derry as part of a large crowd that lined the city pavements for a rather special funeral. My position gave me a perfect view of the event. We stood close to the City and County hospital; the hospital's mortuary was the starting point of the funeral procession. The whispered conversations centred on the death of a young woman at the hands of her husband. Scraps of sentences wafted through the warm summer morning: 'He tried to cut his throat but botched it', 'They found her body out at the Branch', 'He's in a bad way.' Silence fell as the procession came through the hospital gates and along Windsor Terrace on its way to the city cemetery. It was noted that the 'mourning carriage', which followed immediately after the horse-drawn hearse, did not contain the husband. Once the funeral procession passed by, the crowd broke up and went on its way. The *Londonderry Sentinel*, reporting on the funeral, said it was one of the largest seen in the city for many years:

> For a considerable time before the remains left the City and County Hospital at three o'clock, spectators and mourners began to assemble, and in a short time traffic along the route of the procession was practically impossible. Thousands of people lined the route from the Hospital along Marlborough Terrace and Lone Moor Road to the City Cemetery, where countless others had gathered. There were also several hundred in the funeral procession, among them being prominent figures in the public life of the city.

The husband was William Butler, a thirty-one-year-old unemployed insurance salesman, and his wife Jennie Fox was twenty-four. They were married on 26 February of that year, probably just before Lent, when as in Advent, Catholic marriages were as a rule not solemnised. They moved into lodgings in Lower Nassau Street in the west bank of the city, in a district loosely called Rosemount. Jennie died on the Saturday and at the inquest District Inspector Lynn of the Royal Ulster Constabulary (RUC) said that the case was a rare one for Derry. He stated that the Butlers had gone walking on Wednesday night but only William had arrived back. His wife was found on the road next morning, lying in a pool of blood. The husband was later found with his throat gashed, and he was detained under police charge in the hospital.

On 3 September he was charged with the murder of his wife and with his own attempted suicide, then a criminal offence. The accused, 'a slight diminutive figure in a blue suit was led into the court by a police officer, who lifted his hat off for him'. He was not represented by counsel and sat silent during the two-hour hearing. DI Lynn, prosecuting, called Mrs Margaret Mary Coyle, the couple's landlady, as his first witness. She said they had come to live with her at 7 Lower Nassau Street on 27 February, the day after their wedding, and they were quarrelling within a fortnight. They had the front room downstairs with use of the scullery and yard. The quarrels grew in intensity throughout the first couple of weeks in July. On 11 July Mrs Coyle heard the wife say, 'You are a dirty brute and nothing but a pig', and that she would tell her mother about his carry-on. She further reported that, on 12 July, Butler had come into her kitchen asking for face cream 'for a ruffled skin'. She gave him some and next morning asked him about the cream. Butler said it was not for him but for his wife and added: 'We had a bit of a row.' Mrs Coyle insisted that Butler was always very quiet and that, 'Mrs Butler was a very quiet, respectable woman.'

DI Lynn asked her if she had ever heard reference to a third party. The witness replied: 'I did once and Mrs Butler said, "There was nothing with the fellow. He is as good as you. It is just your bad mind."' The couple frequently went walking together. They didn't appear to be on speaking terms on 13 July but they went out in the afternoon. Mrs Coyle saw Butler at 6pm but could not be sure whether Mrs Butler had been there. Butler had gone out again at 9 until 11.30pm. There was no sign of his wife. Next morning a sound described as 'roaring' was heard coming from the Butlers' room and it lasted from 6 until 7.15am. Mrs Coyle knocked at the door and getting no answer opened it. Butler was sitting on the bed in his shirt and trousers and covered in blood. There also was a lot of blood on the floor. 'I said, "Goodness, Willie. What has happened?" He answered, "I must have lost my head, Mrs Coyle." I saw blood coming from a throat wound, and asked him if he cut his throat. He said, "I did."'

Constable M Brennan was called to the house by the Coyles and found Butler lying on his back across the bed. He was conscious and able to respond to the constable's questions. When asked what had happened he repeated that he had lost his head. Regarding his wife's whereabouts, he said, 'We had a row and I left her out the Branch Road.' (The walk was a popular one with Derry people, known as 'going round the Branch'. The usual route was to go out along the Buncrana Road and return by the largely parallel Northland Road, the two being linked by the short Branch Road.) An ambulance was called while Brennan quickly searched the room. He found a safety razor on the mantel piece; both razor and the fireplace were covered with blood. The case was remanded five times before Butler was returned for trial to the Ulster Winter Assizes in December. On his fifth appearance the only witness was Dr James Brewster, assistant house surgeon in the City and County hospital, who gave evidence of Butler's condition on the morning of 14 July:

> [He] was in a shocked and dazed condition when he was admitted at 7.40am. There was an incised wound, five

inches long and one and a half inches deep but no vital artery or vein had been touched and the bleeding had at that time stopped.

He further agreed that the wound could have been self-inflicted and could have been caused by the safety razor blade, which was produced. DI Lynn, who argued the case for the Crown, asked if Butler's condition was that of a man having 'a nervous storm or strain' and Brewster agreed that it was.

Butler was discharged from the City and County on 25 August and returned to Derry Jail. He was customarily silent and never legally represented but sometimes in the days after the killing he would ask about his wife. The details of her death became clear as witnesses were examined at the different hearings. It was another assistant surgeon in the hospital, Dr James A Mark, who revealed the details of Mrs Butler's death. She remained unconscious after she was admitted at 9.20 on the morning of 14 July, eventually dying two days later at 6pm.

> She had three wounds on the back of the scalp, two star-shaped and the other straight — right into the bone. There was no fracture of the skull. Her head was covered with blood. She also had a swelling over the right temple, due to force, and an injury to her eyes that was probably caused by a blow on the temple. There was a scratch across her throat that could have been caused by the rubbing of a scarf.

The post-mortem showed that her brain was congested and swollen as a result of the injuries. It also revealed that she was four months pregnant. The cause of death was due to concussion of the brain and trauma. The bleeding was extensive but not sufficient in itself to cause death. A pair of men's shoes was produced and Mark confirmed that they probably belonged to whoever injured her by repeatedly kicking her in the head.

A picture emerged of severe misalliance from the witnesses'

testimony. A couple of factors contributed to the context behind the tragedy — the cramped living conditions and Butler's unemployment. The confined living conditions might have been more tolerable had he had a job to go to. The couple did their best to mitigate their circumstances by taking frequent walks but it seems that things were wrong from the very beginning. The lack of a honeymoon was not unusual in the Derry of the time. Dr Mark certainly suggests that, in the coarse but effective Ulster phrase, the wedding might have been a 'haddy' (had to) job. We will never know.

Whatever the reason behind their nuptials, there were rows and probably beatings from the start. James Coyle, Mrs Coyle's father-in-law, reported that the Butlers quarrelled two weeks after moving in and occasionally their fights lasted 'fairly well the whole night'. Josephine O'Doherty, of 43 Lower Nassau Street, reported at the first hearing that, on 13 July, on her way to the Labour Exchange, she went through Brooke Park and overtook the Butlers who were walking in the same direction. They did not appear to be on friendly terms with one another and went by separate paths at the city museum. She caught up with them again in Marlborough Street and noticed that Jennie was walking with her head bowed, looking far from happy. Another witness who saw the Butlers that fatal day was Frank Friel, the assistant in Patrick Hegarty's grocery shop on Park Avenue, where they were regular customers. Frank remembered seeing them at 1.30pm and then served Jennie around 4pm; she bought milk and appeared 'quite normal'. He saw them again between 9 and 10pm that evening coming down Upper Nassau Street, the wife walking beside the wall and Willie on the outside.

Frank Molloy, who lived in Glenview Street, which was five minutes from Nassau Street, was a good friend of Willie's, having known him for about fourteen years. He testified to seeing the couple eating apples as they headed for the Moville Road. He met them again at the junction of Glen Road and Northland Road, this time en route to Coshquin, which would take them past the Branch Road. Lynn asked him whether they were walking fast or slow or just like any ordinary couple 'out for a dander'. Molloy chose the third alternative; the use of the 'Ulsterism' by Lynn brought a brief respite to the sombre occasion. John Campbell of Coshquin, a hamlet about three miles from Derry, described returning home from Rosemount that evening. When he reached the British customs post around 11.45pm he thought he heard the cries of an animal in distress. It seemed to come from the continuation of Northland Road, known locally as the middle road, which ran more or less parallel to the Buncrana Road where the customs post was situated. Just then a car passed and he heard no more sounds. Other residents of Coshquin, including Mrs Margaret Burns and her eleven-year-old son, reported that they heard noises similar to those described by Campbell at about 12.10am.

The following morning Vera Clarke, who worked in the Rosemount shirt factory, was walking to work by the middle road. As she approached a spot called Dunne's Brae she saw a body lying in the middle of the road and ran back home to her mother, thinking it was a drunk man. It was the local milkman Joseph Murray who, arriving at 8.30am, found Mrs Butler lying in a pool of blood. In answer to his queries she moaned twice and moved her knee. Murray went to phone for the police and the ambulance. TL Browne, the Sergeant at Pennyburn Police Station on Strand Road, took Murray's call at 8.45am and, with Constables Moran and McSherry, went directly to the scene. He found the woman lying prostrate with her arms by her side. There were two large pools of blood on the road, which seemed to come from a severe injury to the back of the head.

With so much *prima facie* evidence the magistrate, JM King JP, had no hesitation in sending the case to the assizes. The event had generated a lot of 'unhealthy interest'. As the *Derry Journal* of 7 September reported after the hearing of the previous day:

> At the conclusion of the hearing there was a remarkable

scene. A large crowd, including many women and girls, had gathered outside the Courthouse, and when the police van came to convey Butler back to Derry Jail, they swarmed round it, one man mounting the running board. Police had to restrain the crowd, anxious to catch a glimpse of the accused.

The police were preparing for even greater public interest at the trial but their anxiety proved uneccessary.

The *Londonderry Sentinel* of Thursday 17 November put the story rather succinctly:

> How William Butler, aged thirty-one, an unemployed insurance agent who had been in Londonderry Prison since August 25th awaiting trial for the Lovers' Lane murder on July 14th of his wife, a bride of five months, and attempted suicide, dived to his death over a low wall on to a sunken prison road 10ft below was described at the inquest in Londonderry City Hospital on Tuesday.

The *Derry Standard* of Wednesday 16 November gave a full account of the inquest at which Captain JTE Miller, the city coroner, presided. Captain Albert Fryer, the Prisoner Governor, described Butler as a very quiet prisoner who was slow to answer questions and kept very much to himself. There was no indication that he had suicidal tendencies. (A strange comment considering that he had already tried to kill himself.) Then, on Monday 14 November, he was taking his exercise in a place called the wood yard in the company of other prisoners. He was kept clear of them and of all working tools. The wood yard was surrounded by four walls about fifteen feet high. There was a main gate into the yard opposite a low wall, slightly more than two feet in height. On the other side of this wall was a drop of ten feet. Fryer explained that the prisoners had to pass along this wall, adding that they 'had been doing this day and daily, so far as could be ascertained, for about 150 years'. The prisoners lined up in the wood yard, waiting to be brought back to their cells. Butler was at the other end of the yard when he was called. He headed towards the line 'but suddenly he took a dive through the gate and over the wall'.

Dr DE Crosbie, the prison doctor, was summoned and, as he told the inquest, examined the unconscious prisoner in his cell at 12.30pm. He appeared to be suffering from a fracture of the skull and laceration of the brain and Crosbie had him taken to the hospital. Dr Brewster, who had treated Butler for his gashed throat, examined him on arrival at 1.45pm. He was still unconscious. He had a lacerated wound half an inch long on the top of his scalp, two black eyes, and was bleeding from the nose and mouth. He never recovered consciousness and died at 3.20pm the same day.

The last word on Butler's fate was uttered at the Winter Assizes at which he was to be tried for murder and attempted suicide. On 1 December 1938 Lord Justice Best commented: 'Whether it would have been a real murder trial in the sense of trying a man fit to be tried, I cannot say; but at any rate they had nothing to do with him now.'

Almost eleven years later there was a hearing before the Derry assizes that was similar to the Butler case. Gilbert Moffatt, a thirty-three-year-old farmer of Beagh, Gortaclare, Omagh, was charged with the murder of his wife, Ellen Moffatt, on 25 June 1949. He had married Ellen Thompson in 1946 and he and his wife had gone to live with Annie Jordan, an old aunt of his wife, in a house on the main Omagh–Clogher road, somewhat set back from the highway. The lead for the Crown, Edmond Warnock QC, said on Monday 13 December that he couldn't tell the jury much about either of the parties but with certain exceptions which he would detail to them they appeared to have been a reasonably happy couple. The prosecution case was that Moffatt deliberately fired the shots at his wife that killed her. The chief witness for the prosecution was Molly Jordan, Ellen's cousin. (The dead woman was known as Cissie to her family.)

She claimed under oath that on Sunday, 25 June, she had heard two shots and saw Cissie fall. As she fell she cried to her husband, 'Oh, Gilbert,' and he replied, 'Maybe you will stay at home now.'

In a way those seven words made up the whole kernel of the prosecution's case. They implied that Moffatt's defence of accidental death was false. This was further highlighted by the fact that Moffatt immediately reloaded his gun and then shot himself. Molly explained that she called into the house on her way home from Omagh and had tea with the Moffatts and the aunt. She asked her cousin if she had plans for the afternoon but she said, 'How could I go anywhere with my Aunt Annie in bed and him with the big long face?' Moffatt's response was a sort of sneer. Molly said she went out to adjust the saddle of Cissie's bike, and while there she saw the accused with his gun. After the discharge she saw Cissie fall into the flowerbed. When Molly ran for the next-door neighbour she heard another shot. She came out and found Moffatt lying on top of his gun.

This later evidence was corroborated by Dr Hugh Watson of Beragh who said that having arrived at the house of Miss A Jordan at Beagh he had seen a woman lying in a flowerbed. He quickly examined her and found that she was dead. A short distance away he saw the accused lying on his back with a double-barrelled gun beneath him. He was bleeding heavily from a severe wound in the upper left arm. The woman had been shot twice and a post-mortem examination revealed that several ribs had been shattered. Death, due to shock and haemorrhage, had been instantaneous.

As reported by the *Derry Journal*, Warnock suggested to the judge, Lord Justice Porter, 'Would your Lordship think of sending the jury to see the place?' The defence team, E W Jones and J Fox, reckoned it would take about an hour and a half. The judge agreed, saying that it would be beneficial for them to see the house and yard. They were to visit the scene the next morning after breakfast with the necessary escort (Judge Porter was always very wary about what was called then 'jury separation') and the hearing would resume at 2.30pm.

At the hearing Sergeant AO Deignan, of Beragh, read out the statement made to him by the accused on 4 July:

> I was watching for magpies or crows. I had the gun at the hammer and was fixing the bicycle at the same time. They were to go up to George's and Cissie (meaning Mrs Ellen Moffat) would be down with Mollie (her cousin) again. I was still watching for the magpies. They came out and were working about the bicycles. I had the gun in my hand. I was just coming in through the gate by the house. I had the gun in my left hand. I said, 'Are yous away?' Cissie said, 'We are but we won't be long.' I asked Cissie did she get the seat of the bicycle raised as I had forgotten to raise it. I was coming through the gate and she was walking on down by the road. The two hammers were up, and as I was going through the gate, whether I touched the hammers or not, two shots or one went off. I saw Cissie falling in the garden. I could not face the sight.

The Sergeant noted that Moffat said that he wouldn't sign the statement but emphasised he had spoken the truth. Sergeant AL Allen, of the Forensic Department of the Home Office in Preston, examined a photograph of the deceased's body and advised that there were two separate gunshot wounds. He also examined the gun in considerable detail and found it to be in a dangerous condition; the hammers were capable of moving even when it wasn't cocked. He discarded the possibility that the target could have been hit twice, holding the gun in one hand or that it could have been fired by contact with the wire on the gate. He thought it more likely that it had been fired using the trigger. He rejected Jones's suggestion that extraordinary accidents happen with guns, insisting that there is always a reasonable explanation, however 'things do happen on occasions which are extremely difficult to understand'.

The *Londonderry Sentinel* of Thursday, 14 December, reported that on Wednesday the jury travelled sixty miles by bus, escorted by a police car, to Moffatt's home and made an inspection of the house and crime scene.

The speech for the prosecution by Warnock, the Attorney-General, who led for the Crown, strongly implied that Cissie had been accidentally killed by her husband. He suggested Molly Jordan's evidence was ambiguous. Moffat's words, 'Maybe you will stay at home now,' indicated that the shooting was not accidental or unprovoked. There was certainly friction between the couple but he added that they would never now know what caused it. He also said that he had deliberately kept Moffat overlong in the witness box, so that the jury could see what kind of man he was when he was fresh and then when he was tired.

The judge also questioned Jordan's evidence, saying that if it suggested that Moffat intended to kill his wife it did not fit with his sitting down with Cissie and Mollie for tea. He also said that there was no evidence that the accused ever aimed his gun at his wife. The jury decided to take Moffat's word for it that his shotgun had gone off accidentally and that he had no intention of shooting his wife with whom he lived happily. They presented their 'not guilty' verdict after an hour and a half. The charge of attempted suicide remained but Warnock was inclined to be lenient. Formalities, however, had to be carried out. After consulting with Jones, the defence counsel, he suggested that Moffat should now face this second charge of attempted suicide. He pleaded guilty. Warnock suggested it inconceivable that his Lordship punish Moffat for this crime and he himself would not press for any. Jones used the opportunity to comment on matters he had not been able to mention during the trial. He knew his Lordship had seen certain medical reports which made it clear that Moffat 'was not possibly of the alert and advanced mind that certain people might have thought. He had in fact a somewhat backward mind.' He had been in custody since 26 June, admittedly partly in hospital.

Judge Porter agreed that attempted suicide was a very serious crime but, out of respect for Moffat's dreadful experience, and 'particularly having regard to the way in which the Attorney-General had dealt with this charge which was worthy of the highest tradition of the Bar and the administration of law in this country he would not send the accused to jail'. Moffat walked free on the Thursday.

11

JENNIE McCLINTOCK, WILLIAM McCLINTOCK AND HELEN MACKWORTH

Dunmore House is an elegant eighteen-century mansion set in a substantial estate outside the County Donegal village of Carrigans. Situated on a hill, just across the border with County Derry, about five miles from the city, it looks down upon the Foyle and the rich land of County Tyrone. The 500-acre site, which included the village, was first granted in 1620 to house and maintain a plantation dwelling but the present structure dates from 1742. Michael Priestley, the Derry architect who designed so many notable buildings in the northwest of Ireland, clearly had a hand in the planning of Dunmore. One of many striking features of the house, which boasts a detailed Venetian window above a Doric porch, is an especially beautiful walled garden. The estate became the property of the McClintock family on the marriage of William McClintock to the daughter of the original owner, David Harvey, in 1685. William's son John inherited and built the house that exists today.

The McClintocks were well connected, being related to the Alexanders of Caledon, whose famous son would be a leading British general in World War II, becoming a field-marshal and Earl Alexander of Tunis and Errigal when he entered the House of Lords. Another military relation was Alexander's more successful rival Viscount Bernard Montgomery of Alamein. There was also a closer tie by marriage to William Alexander, Bishop of Derry and later Archbishop of Armagh, who married the hymnist Cecil Frances Humphreys, author of 'Once in Royal David's City', 'A Green Hill Far Away' and 'All Things Bright and Beautiful'. The Archbishop's mother, Dorothea McClintock, was brought up as a Presbyterian and then acquiesced in the Anglicanism of her husband, the Rev Robert Alexander, Rector of Garvagh and Aghadowey. Even tenuous kinship links were zealously maintained by the colonising families in the watchful society that persisted from the early seventeenth century

In the 1930s Dunmore was owned by Lieutenant-Colonel Robert McClintock, late of the Royal Engineers, who lived there with his wife Jennie. Their twenty-four-year-old son, and only child, William, continued the family's martial tradition, serving as a second-lieutenant in the Royal Artillery. He got engaged to Helen Mackworth from Sidmouth in Devon; they had met as students. Two years younger than her intended, she was a 'society beauty' and was very much in love with her young subaltern. They were due to marry in June 1938. It was a fairytale romance until tragedy struck that March. William, riding at an army point-to-point, was thrown from his horse. Contrary to gossip at the time, Helen had not encouraged him to ride that day. His spine was shattered, leaving him without any mobility below the chest. He returned to Dunmore as a paraplegic, attended by two English nurses, Dorothy Trotter and Joan Hawkey, who were to provide twenty-four hour care. The wedding was cancelled but Helen accompanied her fiancée back to Ireland, hoping that they might still be married. Her wishes prevailed and a new date was set for Monday, 26 September 1938. The gesture had a kind of defiant nobility about it. She regularly visited Dunmore and busied herself with the wedding preparations.

The Colonel was a man of few words. His approach to life had been tempered by service against the Boers, and the Germans in East Africa during the Great War, and later in India. His household was run with military precision, with breakfast at 9am, lunch at 1pm, afternoon tea at 4pm and dinner at 7pm. Guests were expected to follow their host's example and wear correct evening wear. It was only the Colonel that carved the joint and chose the wine. Dishes were served by the housemaids and conversation at the table was not encouraged. The Colonel usually took his coffee after lunch and dinner alone in his study. His characteristic reserve allowed him to hide the sorrow he must have felt at the family tragedy and he continued to function as normal. His wife Jennie was of a different temperament, however, and could neither conceal her grief at the accident that had effectively ruined her son's life nor hide her dismay at the prospect of the marriage. She made her feelings clear to her husband but tried for the sake of the young couple to hide her anguish. She understood more than the starry-eyed lovers how potentially worrisome their future was likely to be. The one hope she had was that William's life might not be prolonged; his doctors had intimated that he would not enjoy a long life.

On Saturday, 24 September, lunch was served as usual at 1pm. The Colonel and his wife ate in the dining room with the two nurses, who usually dined with the family. William had been carried into the walled garden where he and Helen took lunch on sunny days. It was Mrs McClintock's usual practice in good weather to bring the coffee out to her son. That Saturday she left almost immediately followed by Helen, who declared that she felt slightly unwell. Mrs McClintock advised the servants that Helen had gone to her room and was not to be disturbed. At 1.50pm the Colonel was in his study getting ready to take Joan Hawkey into town when he heard two gunshots. He wasn't especially startled since Helen and his wife regularly shot at pigeons with a .22 rifle. Before heading off he went into the garden to say goodbye to William. To his utter horror he found his son unconscious and covered with blood; there was blood coming from his mouth, running down his neck, soaking his shirt and jacket. He thought that William was haemorrhaging and ran to fetch Dorothy Trotter, the nurse on duty. (Joan Hawkey was upstairs in her attic room dressing to go out.)

At the inquest, held in the Colonel's study that same evening,

Dorothy Trotter reported that the Colonel had come running from the walled garden, shouting, 'Sister, William is bleeding from the mouth. Will you come out to the garden?' He then jumped in his car to get the family physician and friend, Dr William Rankin, telling the nurses to find his wife.

Dorothy Trotter ran to William and knew at once that he was dead. She quickly determined to break the news to Mrs McClintock before she could see her son's body. She sent Joan, who had joined her, to strike the gong to summon the mistress and Helen but there was no response. 'We then thought that Mrs McClintock and Miss Mackworth had discovered that William was dead and had gone off together to console each other.' Dorothy remained with William. As she reported at the inquest, 'I walked up and down by the body, and nearby I noticed a weeding glove lying on the ground. Workmen then came on the scene and had William's body removed to the house.' The glove, which belonged to Mrs McClintock, had absolutely no relevance in the case but it was the kind of detail that tends to fix itself in the memory in moments of extremity. Dorothy and Maggie Bradley, one of the maids, searched the grounds for Mrs McClintock and made a grim discovery in the tool-shed. They found her body 'behind the rushes'; her head had been partially blown away and a single-bore shotgun lay between her legs. It was a horrible sight and as Dorothy put it, 'The maid who was with me, Maggie Bradley, went into hysterics.'

Meanwhile Helen had left her room, having been disturbed by all the noise. She approached the nurses and asked what was wrong. When they broke the news to her she was visibly shocked, whispering, 'I don't know how I will live without him.' They took her back to her room and persuaded her to lie down again. By now the Colonel and Dr Rankin had arrived back at Dunmore. It took only a few minutes to conclude that William had been fatally shot. Dorothy Trotter had to then tell the distraught father that his wife was also dead. The two men went to the tool-shed to attend to her when Joan Hawkey suddenly burst in crying, 'Quick, quick, doctor; come quick. Helen is still alive. She has shot herself.' Dorothy Trotter described how she and Joan Hawkey heard another gunshot: 'Together we ran to Master William's room, where I found Miss Mackworth lying on the floor and bleeding profusely from the right temple, nose and mouth.' There was a .22 rook rifle lying on the floor by the bed. Helen died in great pain at 3.45pm with Nurse Trotter by her side until the end.

By now officers of what were still called then the Civic Guards had arrived. It is hard to imagine the terror and misery experienced that day. In the space of two hours on a warm, sunny afternoon, three people had died; one murdered and two by suicide.

Dr Rankin reported at the inquest that the left side of Mrs McClintock's head had been completely blown away 'seemingly by a gunshot'. The surrounding area was splattered with brain matter. He described how the fatal shot was fired: 'the gun must have been discharged while the deceased was in a standing position and the gun leaned against the window of the toolshed'. He also described how he had found young McClintock with a gaping wound, about two-and-a-half inches in diameter, on the top of the head: 'Brain matter was exuding from the wound, which was evidently caused by a gunshot fired at fairly close range.' Helen's death had been caused by a gunshot to her right temple in front of the ear. He explained that there was no hope for her by the time he got to her.

Inevitably the chief focus at the inquest was on Jennie McClintock. Her reaction to her son's accident and the impact it had on her dominated the proceedings. Joan Hawkey had noticed signs of stress when she first met Mrs McClintock in London. She told the coroner that she felt the stress to stem from shock at her son's recent invalided condition. When she returned to Dunmore she improved but as the date of the wedding drew near her mood darkened again. She was unable to sleep and prowled about the house at night. Her behaviour could be erratic; she talked loudly, making little sense. The discreet household staff treated her as normal, thinking that she would probably improve once William was married and the fuss had died down. She had been in a decidedly disturbed state on the Friday, dreading the wedding celebration. The house was buzzing in preparation for the big day; tables were being laid out for the celebratory breakfast and the many wedding presents were on display. The marriage of the only child of an important family was a significant social event despite the shadow hanging over it and the unspoken realisation that William was going to be the last of the McClintock line.

Mrs McClintock had been born in the Punjab in 1885, the daughter of Sir George Casson Walker, who was administrator of British railways in India. She met Robert in India when she helped nurse him through a long illness. As the popular lady of the manor, she frequently visited the homes of the tenants and distributed seasonal gifts. One of the tenants described her to the *Derry Journal* as having a kind and sweet nature. All changed, however, after her William's accident: 'She was rarely seen in the village or at the church at which she had previously been a constant attender.'

The last few days of her life were described at the inquest in the house, which began at 9pm and finished by candlelight after midnight. Present were material witnesses, a jury of six, Chief Superintendent McManus and Superintendent Munnelly from Letterkenny, WT McMenamin, State Solicitor, and Dr Sarsfield Kerrigan, coroner for East Donegal. All were conscious of the three corpses in the room above and the wedding cake and gifts in the dining room across the hall.

Colonel McClintock was called first. He entered the room with something of his old military bearing but was clearly grief-stricken. In a voice scarcely above a whisper he wished those present, 'Good night.' To save him further pain the coroner proposed to read his statement that he had made earlier. In it the Colonel described how he had gone to Derry on business that morning, returning between noon and 1pm. He saw William in the walled garden and then spoke to his wife. Her behaviour since the accident had been neurotic; the shock of the accident had been bad enough but the couple's insistence on going ahead with the wedding was equally painful. That day, however, according to her husband's written testimony, she seemed slightly less depressed than usual. They lunched together and then the Colonel went to his study while she headed for the garden. Her behaviour over the previous few days — the loud talking and nocturnal walks — had worried the two nurses. They told her that she needed to pull herself together because she was upsetting William. They gave her a sleeping draught and that morning she appeared to be in better shape.

The coroner asked some necessary questions as sensitively as he could 'for the sake of getting things cleared up. I suppose it was only natural that she should be distressed on account of her poor boy. Previous to this date did she ever show signs of any likelihood to do any deliberate harm either to herself or anybody else?' The Colonel replied that she used to talk very wildly at times 'and within the last three months she certainly thought it would be a good thing if she and I would commit suicide, having previously killed my son. I thought that she was raving and told her not to be so silly and it passed off. I must say I did not think she seriously meant it. She had not been sleeping at all for some time past.' The Colonel also told the hearing that she had been involved in a bad road accident: 'While motoring she was driven broadside on into another car. She received a bad cut on the head, which may have had something to do with her condition.' He believed she was heading for a severe mental breakdown, 'which must have come today. The whole time she was getting worse and worse. She did not go out to see anybody.'

After the nurses gave their evidence the jury retired to deliberate the matter, returning thirty minutes later with the inevitable verdict that Mrs McClintock, while temporarily insane, fired a shot at her son, killing him, and that she then committed suicide, and that Miss Mackworth also committed suicide while temporarily insane. Dr Kerrigan, concluding with an apology for the lateness of the hour, said he wished to extend the sympathy of the people to the Colonel: 'I will only say, as one Christian gentleman to another, that God may give strength to stand your ordeal. It is really too great a tragedy to say much about.' Superintendent Munnelly, on behalf of the Guards, associated himself with the coroner's sympathy, as did Mr George Wilkin, the foreman, on behalf of the jury. The Colonel quietly thanked the men for their words. The dark day had come to an end.

The Rev David Kelly, Rector of Glendermott in Derry and incumbent in charge of Killea church in Carrigans, was to officiate at William and Helen's wedding. He held his usual Sunday service the day before the funerals and used the opportunity to dilate upon the virtues of Mrs McClintock. He spoke of her active interest in the welfare of the parish and of her work for the Donegal Protestant Orphan's Society, including her sponsorship of a special appeal to be sent to all the parishes for an increase in subscriptions. His closing words were an attempt to ease the bitterness of the grief: 'It is a tragedy and triumph of love: the bond of love was stronger than the thread of life.'

The funeral took place on what should have been William's twenty-fifth birthday, Monday, 26 September, and was a low-key affair. The three coffins were taken separately by motor hearse on the short journey from Dunmore House to the church. Helen's body was conveyed first, then William's and finally that of the tragic mother. They were carried by tenants and placed side by side on the chancel steps. The organist, Miss D Gailey, played 'How Bright These Glorious Spirits Shine' by Isaac Watts, with its poignant third verse,

> Hunger and thirst are felt no more
>   Nor suns with scorching ray.

> God is their sun, whose cheering beams
>> Diffuse eternal day.

Among the mourners were Mrs McClintock's nephew, DI Landale, who walked with Colonel McClintock, Dr Rankin, Superintendent Munnelly, Rev JK Beattie, Rector of Taughboyne, the adjoining parish, and Lt-Col Gledstanes, a friend of the Colonel's. Some of the congregation were wedding guests.

The service was conducted by Rev Kelly. Psalm 103, with its stark words, 'As for man his days are as grass: as a flower of the field, so he flourisheth. For the wind passeth over it and it is gone; and the place thereof shall know it no more,' was followed by the Office of the Dead. Then the coffins were carried out to the graveyard, past the little schoolhouse that William had attended as a young boy. 'The Sands of Time Are Sinking' by Anne Ross Cousin was the recessional hymn. Mother and son were interred in the McClintock family plot while Helen was placed a few feet away in a new part of the cemetery. The graves were decorated with dahlias, sweet-pea, asters and mixed laurels and ivy, a spontaneous embellishment by some of the McClintock tenants. A brief committal service was carried out by the Rev Kelly. Colonel McClintock, who had remained impassive throughout, finally broke down as he stood between the two graves.

The events of that awful September were felt by many. Dorothy Trotter continued with her nursing career and had a long and interesting life. Nevertheless, she admitted to suffering from recurrent psychological strain for many years afterwards. The concept of post-traumatic stress had not been formalised in those years. She only ever discussed the tragedy in detail with her husband. Therefore, her two daughters expressed some reservations about her publishing her memoirs, entitled *Trotting Through Life*, in 1985, in which she recalled the awful events. She visited Ireland in 1981 and again in 1995 as an octogenarian at the invitation of local historian and broadcaster Ken

McCormick. He accompanied her on a return visit to Dunmore House.

In her autobiography she wrote that she still had difficulty accepting the McClintock tragedy. She believed that if she had locked the bedroom in which William's body had been laid then Helen would not have seen the remains of her fiancé and, therefore, might not have shot herself: 'She was sitting on the bed looking over her wedding presents and when I talked to her about William she burst into tears and told me that she could not live without him.' One other poignant detail recalled by her was the instruction to shoot Blarney, Helen's dog, so that it could be buried with her. It was then that Dorothy broke down in tears. She took her companion through the garden, described her search for Mrs McClintock and told how she almost tripped over the body. Her visit to Dunmore may have been intended as a kind of exorcism but in fact the visit led to a further bout of psychosomatic illness, confirming her daughters' reservations about her return to Ireland. She died in 2004 aged ninety-two.

Colonel McClintock remained in Dunmore House. He spent his days quietly, constructing ornamental fencing and trelliswork in the tool-shed until his death on 11 July 1943. The house still commands its Priestley dignity, its elegant façade betrays no sign of the triple tragedy from almost seventy years earlier.

12
MARY McGOWAN

WHEN ON HOLY SATURDAY, 16 April 1949, Mary McGowan staggered into the garden at the back of her house, at 18 Ponsonby Avenue, in North Belfast, it was too late for medical attention. Minnie, as she was known to her neighbours, had suffered near strangulation from the doubled cord still looped round her neck and there were so many stab wounds to her face, arms and neck that two children, the five-year-old Rafferty twins, did not recognise the 'red lady' as being Mrs McGowan, their neighbour who had drunk tea with their mother less than an hour before. Minnie's assailant had tried to strangle her manually, as well as with the rope, and had repeatedly stabbed her with her own carving knife. Then he smashed a mineral water bottle full of holy water over her head, poured boiling soup on her wounded face, all the while kicking and punching her. When he finally left he turned on the gas at the cooker.

Dr Lynch, who tended her at the Mater Infirmorum Hospital, at the foot of the Crumlin Road, read a statement at the trial, summarising her many injuries. The pedestrian language highlights the savageness of the attack:

> She was suffering from extensive laceration to the skull, which took the form of multiple incised wounds. These could have been caused by a knife or broken bottle. There was a large wound and several incised wounds on the head, also an incised wound to the right ear and an incised wound near the mouth. She was bleeding from the mouth and both ears, and her nose was fractured. Her face was

swollen, her lips bluish and both eyes closed. Her tongue
was swollen. There was a small wound on the right hand
and left forefinger. There were bruises on the back and to
both hands and her neck. There were extensive burns to
the face and neck and both arms. There were bruises on the
legs. The cause of death was secondary shock, the result of
having received multiple bruises, severe loss of blood,
severe burns, aggravated by attempted strangulation.

Dr Lynch was one of several people to whom the dying woman whispered the name of her attacker, 'Robert the Painter.'

She managed to tell her appalled neighbours that she was dying, and fretted about her only child, Kathleen, who was visiting an ailing relative in south County Armagh, and her husband who was ill in hospital: 'Kathleen's in Newry... I'm dying... Don't let her come here... I'm going to die... Poor Daddy, he'll get a terrible shock.' Her self-diagnosis was a significant point for the killer's defence team. It was also sadly accurate; by Easter Monday the charge of attempted murder became absolute.

The Belfast of the period was relatively free from overt sectarianism. This was partly due to war weariness (the Luftwaffe had been unselective in its targeting) but mostly because both sides of the sectarian divide in the North benefited equally from the welfare legislation of the post-war Attlee government. (Not all Unionist politicians approved; there was considerable opposition to the generous family allowances because they said Catholics with their much larger families would benefit more that loyal Protestants.) Ulster, as it was inaccurately labelled by the majority, had the free medical services and the education opportunities available in other parts of the UK. People in the newly designated Republic of Ireland (declared on 18 April 1949, the day Minnie died) envied their northern brethren their economic advantages.

There was little to disturb the civil order. The Orange Order held its summer walks, often through nationalist areas. The Apprentice Boys of Derry had a different colour — the strident Derry crimson — for their two celebrations: the shutting of the city gates on 18 December and the 12 August commemoration for the ending of their famous siege. The first of these involved the burning in explosive effigy of the cruelly traduced Colonel Lundy. The nationalist citizens of the maiden city showed then no serious objection to what became a pre-Christmas event and the 'relief' ceremonies were attended by some excellent bands of the sort that caused the heart of the Ulster poet, Louis MacNeice, to leap as he wrote in his poem, 'Valediction'.

In its industrial twilight Belfast still bore the scars of the airraids, though these were slightly mitigated by thick growths of rosebay willow herb, or fireweed. Whistles sounded throughout the city, summoning workers to factories and yards that puffed up smoky columns from their tall chimneys.

As Maurice Craig, the place's unacknowledged laureate, put it, Belfast was 'knocked up from the swamp in the last hundred years'. Yet it *was* a city; it had trams, trolleys and buses. It needed them since few people had cars; petrol was rationed, as were sweets. In fact rationing did not finally end till 1955. It had two working theatres, Frank Matcham's Opera House, with its sign 'Through this door pass the most beautiful girls in the world', and the Empire, not counting the little Group, an adjunct of the Ulster Hall in Bedford Street. If one could scrape together a halfcrown, one could see ballet, West End shows and sometimes classical theatre, presented most often by the egregious Donald Wolfit, his wife Rosalind Iden, and a rag, tag and bobtail of strolling players.

The city had more than a score of cinemas, many of which were palatial. Films were listed in the *Belfast Telegraph*, then strongly unionist in its politics but read by sporting nationalists because it printed the horse-race results and the 'cards' for the Celtic and Dunmore greyhound races. Similiarly, Protestants bought the nationalist *Irish News*, founded in 1891 as an anti-

Parnellite morning paper, because it frequently, and successfully, predicted racing outcomes at home and abroad. It later rivalled the *News Letter*, its unionist equivalent, as the chief voice of constitutional anti-partitionism. There were also many dance halls, ranging from pocket-size tuition studios like John Dossor's and Billy Neely's to the opulent Orpheus and Plaza, with the very popular Club Orchid somewhere in between. Then there was the glamorous Floral Hall under Cave Hill that seemed to be all windows, and from where, on clear nights, you could see the lights on Belfast Lough. Across the bay, around the corner to the east, was Ballyholme where the combined dance and bus ticket for Caproni's got you to 'Bangor and back for a bob.' Quicksteps were danced, as were foxtrots, slow waltzes, tangos, sambas and the more complicated moonlight saunter. The best combination, particular to nationalist halls, was céilí and old time, guaranteed to please everybody. Though the city looked like Calvin's Geneva on the Sabbath, with children's swings tied up in case someone had fun, there was a subversive element. In venues like Fruithill tennis club or Newington parish hall one could dance on a Sunday night and, on nights of clement weather, the Falls Road from the Royal Victoria Hospital to the Glen Road provided a *paseo* that rivalled the one Derry students experienced at home on Carlisle Road.

The reason for this portrait of the city is to emphasise how peaceful it was. Serious crime was minimal and one walked freely all over town, day and night. The convoluted trials of Robert the Painter attracted about as much attention as the Korean War, which was very little indeed. The case seemed open and shut. After all, the victim had named her assailant.

Ponsonby Avenue was a street of fine terrace houses with gardens out back. The street had suffered in the April and May German air raids eight years earlier, but the even-numbered houses had escaped. In spite of gross discrimination in government jobs, the higher civil service, consultancies in all NHS hospitals, top ranks in the police force and fire service, and senior posts in BBC Northern Ireland, there was a developing Catholic middle class. The area was mixed but tolerant. The complex of streets that included Ponsonby was located just at the point where the Antrim Road's wealthier inhabitants lived. It was bounded on the southwest by the respectable Duncairn Gardens and on the northeast by the Limestone Road. Both of these streets ran down to the Protestant York Street, enclosing the enclave known as 'Tiger's Bay', after the dockland area of Cardiff.

Tiger's Bay included Meadow Street, where the apprentice decorator Robert lived, and Lilliput Street, where Lily, his complaisant girlfriend, lived. The upper ends of Duncairn Gardens and the Limestone Road contained the Catholic parish of Newington, the location for Sunday night dances. Across the Antrim Road were Cliftonville and Cavehill Roads, the latter fronting the waterworks. It's not difficult to imagine that the working-class Protestants might have resented the uppity 'Taigs' who lived in these upper-class areas — though the area actually had a majority of Protestants.

The McGowans were quiet people who got on well with their Protestant neighbours and frequently employed Protestant firms for jobs about the house. This was how Robert was first introduced to the McGowan household. John McGowan ran a busy pub, the Waldorf, so the domestic details were his wife's concern. Over the four years from 1944 to 1948 Robert Taylor did four 'wee jobs' for Mrs McGowan. Their acquaintance was limited but Taylor's boyish good looks were sufficiently striking to be memorable, even if the standard of the 'wee jobs' wasn't.

The truth was that Taylor was lacking, both as a personality and workman. He had left Fane Street Primary School at thirteen after a history of repeated truancy. The school was a considerable distance from his home, more than two miles to the south, but in a district as intensely loyalist as Tiger's Bay, known as the 'Village'. There followed a series of short-term jobs, which he left with a reputation for dishonesty and actual thievery.

Nevertheless, he secured an apprenticeship with a plumber whose business was sited on the Antrim Road, convenient to his home. He didn't stay long and next got a job in a nursery on Malone Road but had to leave after a month under suspicion for pilfering. He was now fourteen years of age and his next job seemed to promise better. He worked for a linen company for a year until he was suspected of stealing from the company's payroll and duly sacked.

Fortunately the company decided not to bring charges and he was soon apprenticed to Barretts in the now vanished Sunnyside Street, just off the Limestone Road. It seemed a desirable placement. He began with a wage of £1 a week, rising by an annual increment of £1 until after five years when he would be 'out of his time' and able to earn £5 a week, not an insubstantial sum at the time. He would then have been a fully professional painter and decorator and be entitled to the sobriquet that clung to him in the autumn of 1949 and spring of 1950. However, Barrett was forced to sack him in February 1949 after three customers complained about his possible thievery.

Contrary to decent business practice, he tried to poach clients from his old employer. He called into residents at Ponsonby Avenue, trying to persuade them that he had finished his apprenticeship (a lie) and was hoping to set up his own business (a fantasy). The McGowans gave him short shift, telling him that they preferred to stay with Mr Barrett. Robert stormed away in frustration, slamming the front gate. The rejection added to his store of resentment against the woman who was always so critical of his work and constantly nagged that he clean up after himself.

He was desperate for money.

Like many of his peers he believed that he was naturally superior to any 'Fenian'. He resented the criticisms of his sloppy work by what he perceived to be an old crone. Minnie was only in her mid-fifties but probably appeared much older to the young Robert. Perhaps it was the combination of age resentment and sectarian hatred that finally proved too much. What else could explain the prolonged savagery of the attack? The case was utterly shocking for Catholic and Protestant alike. The city had not become hardened to the killing that was to characterise it twenty years later.

Whatever about the nationalist perception of the RUC as a sectarian, partial police force they were in fact highly efficient. Just sixty minutes after the murder a standard police issue Wolseley car pulled up outside 13 Lower Meadow Street, containing the uniformed DI Hugh Davis and the plain-clothed Detective Head Constable Thornton. When Robert came to the door they explained that they were making enquiries about a serious assault committed upon Mrs Minnie McGowan of Ponsonby Avenue. Robert denied any complicity and offered a hastily contrived alibi. His description of his Saturday morning was reasonably convincing, if he could prove it. He said that he had called at the Daisy, the newsagents in York Street, the arterial road that ran by Belfast Lough and, parallel to the Antrim Road, acted as the eastern boundary of the Protestant stronghold. It was here that he had the *Irish News* on order because, as a dedicated punter, he depended upon the paper's greyhound tipster for his intermittently successful gambling. He used a shop sufficiently remote to prevent his neighbours finding out that he read a 'Fenian rag'. The implicit paranoia shown here was symptomatic of his personal inadequacy; any decent betting man wanted the best information on the dogs. The *Irish News* correspondent had an excellent reputation and no 'Prod' punter would have missed his forecasts, any more than a 'Taig' would have failed to buy at least one of the *Belfast Telegraph*'s three evening editions.

Robert was now relying on the cooperation of George Clarke, the Daisy's proprietor, to say that he had called to pick up his paper. The other peg on which he hoped to hang his false alibi required the connivance of his betting friend, Billie Booth, who worked as a cleaner at the City Hall. He claimed that he sought out Billie because he had leant him £5 some time ago and now needed it back to defray some of the expenses for his upcoming wedding.

Anyone could understand how desperation over shortage of money might drive Robert to rob a 'prosperous' housewife like Minnie McGowan but it would require a criminal psychologist to explain the relentless savagery of the attack.

The character of Lily Jones, the accommodating girlfriend, is hard to bring into focus. She must have been happy enough to indulge Taylor's sexual needs, however uncomfortable the location. Since both the houses in Meadow Street and Lilliput Street were small and crowded they must have spent some time in the shrubbery of the locked Alexandra Park. Whatever the location Lily got pregnant and it was decided that they should be married as soon as possible.

The two families fixed the wedding date for Easter Monday, 18 April 1949. It was a popular date for weddings; both the Catholic and Protestant Churches did not 'solemnise nuptial feasts', to use the liturgical phrase, during Lent or Advent. It didn't give Taylor much time to prepare, he had to find money urgently. There was the ring, the licence, the breakfast and transportation, and he had no job! Lily's father was unemployed and Taylor in manic mode, perhaps to compensate for the pregnancy, assured him that he would pay all the expenses. Earlier in the month he had come to an arrangement with a taxi firm who said they would supply four cars, two bouquets, four ladies sprays and three buttonholes for £12. The taxi journeys would have been quite short since the chosen church, St Barnabas, was not far away, further down Duncairn Gardens. (Neither Taylor nor Lily was a regular churchgoer but the minister of St Barnabas' was persuaded to hold the service.) With his usual mixture of optimism and self-delusion Taylor listened to the owner of the taxi firm's suggestions and faithfully promised to pay the fee on the Saturday before the wedding.

Taylor's occasional gambling success had led to large claims about the money that he saved. There was a period in 1948 when his winnings were greater than his losses; it was during the final months of his apprenticeship and he was earning £3 a week, which allowed him to bet in pounds rather than shillings. He also claimed that he had inherited £6,000 but no one, except possibly Lily, believed him. When the time came to plan the wedding he had only £30 in the post office and most of that had been lost in another unsuccessful night in Dunmore Park. He became obsessed about money.

Minnie McGowan would be sure to have money in the house, especially now that her husband John was ill in hospital. The problem was that he would be immediately suspected if money went missing from the house. Already in his mind the need for her death was taking shape. But Minnie put up a brave fight.

The detectives had plenty of evidence of a struggle. There was blood found on his sock and foot during the forensic examination in Glenravel Street police station. Detective Head Constable Thornton asked him to change into other clothes. He also asked him if he knew Mrs McGowan of Ponsonby Avenue. Robert replied that he had not been near the house in over a year. Thornton then asked him about the five scratches on his face and Taylor claimed that they had been caused by his sister's youngest child, sustained while he played with him. He was also questioned about the red stains on the sleeve of his coat and on the knees and the left turn-up of his trousers. There was plenty to connect him with the offence and he was charged with attempted murder and then murder after Minnie died.

The defence tried to present an innocent explanation for the bloodstained clothes, claiming that Taylor had a susceptibility to paint that led to nosebleeds. They also urged that Minnie McGowan's identification of her assailant should be inadmissible. When her statement was eventually allowed they tried to argue that her not asking for a priest when she believed herself to be dying implied that her mind was unhinged and therefore her identification of Taylor unreliable. At the preliminary hearing, at the end of May, most of Taylor's statements about his movements on the day of the murder proved untrue. His last visit to Ponsonby Avenue was shown to be in February and not, as he claimed, more than a year earlier. Mrs Mary Shiels, who lived at number twenty-eight, had seen him in Atlantic Avenue, the street that lay at right angles to Ponsonby Avenue, on the morning of the sixteenth and readily identified him in the line-up. His assertion that he had been to the Daisy on York Road to pick up his *Irish News* on the Saturday morning was rejected by the proprietor George Clarke. Likewise Billie Booth denied that he owed Taylor any money and insisted that he had not seen him on the morning of the murder.

With such overwhelming evidence and the existence of hairs, fibres and blood that connected Taylor to his victim, the magistrate automatically referred the case to the Crown Court. Yet Taylor's preternatural luck held. He and Minnie McGowan both had O-type blood. If it could be shown that their blood groups differed, the public and the legal system would be spared a farrago of specious argument. Another significant and much more crucial element in the case was the looming prospect of capital punishment. In the relatively crime-free province hangings were rare events. The last case was that of the IRA man Tom Williams, who was hanged in 1942 for shooting a policeman. As a result nobody believed that Taylor would hang. The Governor-General of Northern Ireland, as representative of the King, had the power to commute the death sentence to life imprisonment. Cynics (and in the circumstances there were many) were interested not in whether but how he would escape the hangman. Meanwhile, the crowds in the courtroom strongly hinted that the Protestant population of Belfast, not just of Tiger's Bay, had closed ranks. The hostile witnesses, Mrs Rafferty and Mr Skillen, the neighbours who rendered what aid they could to Minnie, and Mrs Shiels were attacked verbally as 'Fenian liars' and the totally intrusive and illogical Twelfth parade around Newington made a lot of noise when it passed by 18 Ponsonby Avenue.

The progress of Taylor's trials preoccupied the Belfast papers, especially the *Irish News* and the *News Letter*. West of the Bann and on the other side of the Glenshane Pass there was less interest and coverage. On Wednesday, 2 June, the *Derry Standard* carried a paragraph in one of the inner pages, stating that 'Robert Taylor, a 21-year-old painter of Meadow Street, Belfast, was charged with the alleged murder of Minnie McGowan, aged 52 of 18 Ponsonby Avenue.' On 4 June, the next edition of the paper (it was published three times a week) carried an unconnected story that was to play a part in the tale: 'Because the father of an accused man was seen speaking to a juryman at Londonderry County Crown Sessions on Thursday, Judge Copeland discharged the jury, saying that a trial under such circumstances would be a farce.'

Robert the Painter's trial began on 25 July before Justice Sheil. In the crowded courtroom some of the Catholic audience noticed that the foreman of the jury was a grocer who had a shop at the end of Halliday's Road where it met Duncairn Gardens. He was an acquaintance of Taylor; indeed he had refused him his first job as message boy. It is not unlikely that his was the decisive voice in the first trial's verdict — more than adequate compensation for the earlier slight. Research by Tom McAlindon, author of *Bloodstains in Ulster*, reveals that only one of the twelve jurymen was against the guilty verdict. The lead for the Crown was Lancelot Curran KC MP, former Attorney-General, the youngest in the province's history, for nearly three years. He was a relentless cross-examiner and destined for higher things in his profession. Defending Taylor was George Hanna, another bright spark in his profession, who had political ambitions as well. The case seemed hopeless but he had nothing to lose by defending a working-class lad from Tiger's Bay. Hanna dressed his client and his witnesses with the care of a theatre director. Robert, transmogrified into Bobby — a younger and sweeter name — was dressed with care in a suit and open-necked shirt to emphasise his youthful good looks and implicit innocence. Lily was dressed in black and Hanna allowed her to appear on stage only when it suited his needs. The growing evidence of her pregnancy could also be used to dramatic advantage.

Hanna needed all the stratagems he could muster. Curran was a formidable adversary and quickly demolished Taylor's alibis. The over-elaborate detail of Taylor's fake visit to the Daisy was a giveaway. He claimed that he had given George Clarke a three-penny piece and received two pence change. His suggestion that Clarke keep the paper until 6pm when he wasn't so busy was an obvious lie. Clarke's denial and Billie Booth's refusal to back up his story about the loan effectively wiped out his alibi.

There was another defence witness, a volunteer, whose obviously false evidence didn't help Taylor's case. It was not clear whether Mary Walker's offer of taking the stand was rooted in solidarity with a fellow denizen of the Bay or whether her appearance was just another of the mysterious elements that characterised the case. She knew the accused well but had not heard until Easter Tuesday that he had been arrested. She was prepared to swear that she had seen him in High Street at 12.20pm on the crucial Saturday morning. This was a surprise to the police who had not been given the information and indeed it had not been mentioned when she visited Taylor with his parents. She said she had been on the bus with her daughter and saw Robert wearing 'a heavy blue overcoat, the belt was hanging loose… I nodded to him and he nodded back.' Her story unfortunately contradicted another hastily contrived alibi involving Lily and her sister that placed him at her house at 12.25pm. It is interesting that Lily, Taylor senior or Mary Walker were never arraigned for their patent perjury.

The trial lasted four days, closing on 28 July. After the summings-up by counsel and judge the jurymen were dismissed at 6pm to consider their verdict. A quick decision was expected; in the phrase of the day 'the very dogs in the street knew that

Taylor was guilty' but juries have to consider the arguments for and against and the phrase 'beyond a reasonable doubt' may have burdened some more than others. In fact they did not emerge until 9.40pm and then without a verdict. The American legal practice of permission to 'poll the jury' — asking each for his verdict — was not available and the acceptance of majority decisions was not introduced until 1967. A vastly relieved Taylor was led away to face a new and final trial on 24 October. There was jubilation among Taylor's band of loyal supporters both in the courtroom and outside it. The enhanced persona of 'Robert the Painter' was beginning to emerge.

The summer and autumn with their Orange and Crimson walks and the beginning of the academic year passed quietly and for a while Taylor was moved to the margin of the public's awareness. Yet when the second and, by law, final trial began on Monday 24 October Protestant Belfast was agog with interest again. Seats in the court were at a premium and local press coverage was intense. Curran came out fighting and had no difficulty in destroying the credibility of the defence witnesses; this time the jury brought a guilty verdict in less than thirty minutes.

The *Derry Standard* carried the story of the sentence in a six-inch single-column story on an inside page, recording that the all-male jury took thirty-five minutes to reach the guilty verdict. (In fact the actual time was thirty-nine minutes.) The hanging was fixed for Wednesday, 16 November, exactly seven months after the murder. The full panoply of black cap, placed on the judge's wig by the Court Crier, was noted but the readers were spared the full grisly formula with its dire phrases: 'the common place of execution', 'hanged by the neck until you are dead' and 'buried within the walls of the prison'. The paper headed the piece 'Belfast Death Sentence' with a subhead, 'No Appeal Lodged Yet' and noted that an appeal could be lodged at any time within ten days.

The trial ended on Friday 28 October and Hanna lodged his

appeal on the following Monday. He had two bases for appeal: the admission of the dying woman's identification of her killer as evidence and the 'scandalous' behaviour of the jury during the second trial. The first was weak; in fact its acceptability had been effectively ruled upon by the Lord Chief Justice, Sir James Andrews KC. The second was more serious but reeked of contrivance. During the second trial in October the jury had been granted permission to break their isolation. Neilson, the Under-Sheriff of the city, who had charge of the jurors, said on their behalf that they were feeling the strain of the court sessions and would like a trip to Bangor for physical refreshment. (A similar request had been made and granted during the July trial.) Andrews reluctantly assented on the condition that the jurymen be accompanied by four RUC men, two to lead and two to follow behind, and one of the officers should be, at least, a sergeant.

These conditions were not meticulously followed. John Woods, the foreman, instructed the bus driver to drive not to Bangor but the further six miles to Donaghadee. The party arrived at 8.00pm and separated into three groups. Sergeant Rouse, the designated officer, accompanied six of the twelve to a pub. The room they chose had two other drinkers who left before there was any possibility of conversation. This group returned to the bus about 9.00pm after three rounds of drinks. Three others, with Constable Malcolm, took a ten minute walk along the front but found the windy October weather unpleasant and joined the other constables with their three good men in a seaside café which was empty apart from the waitress. By 9.00pm all twelve were back in the bus and back at the court by 10.00pm. The integrity of the jury was scarcely scratched on that trip.

This time the excursion was to Antrim. Only nine wished to take advantage of the permission to travel and the rest stayed in the jury's room at the courthouse. One of the constables had to remain with them. Arriving at Antrim three members strolled with Constable Malcolm along the long, broad main street before repairing to a coffee shop for pastries. Sergeant Rouse went with three to Hall's Hotel for drinks. Again they had no extraneous conversation. The same was true with Constable Stewart's three who had stopped at a fruit shop and, though there was some desultory conversation with other purchasers, the trial was not discussed. On the way home Foreman Woods directed the driver to go by the Limestone Road and Atlantic Avenue, allowing them to glance up Ponsonby and view the scene of the crime.

There was no moral evidence of jury 'separation' but there was a technicality that the Machiavellian Hanna could begin to work on. Further he could assume that the twelve and their police escorts would unlikely be subject to cross-questioning by the appeal judges, Lord Justices Porter and Black, or the new Attorney-General, JE Warnock KC MP. He began with a reference to the 'view' of Ponsonby of which three jurors had been deprived. (Warnock later dismissed this complaint as trivial: it was dark and the bus did not stop.) Hanna made much more of the 'separation' issue, even though it was clear that there had been only a formal transgression and no real infringement. (Judge Copeland, in his dismissal of the Derry jury on 4 June, was defending a principle of jury integrity, a protection for both defence and prosecution. This was light years from the legerdemain practised by the wily Hanna.) Warnock attempted to dismiss this too, arguing that there had been no actual 'separation'. The two appeal judges, especially Porter, took a sterner view. He delivered his judgement on 20 January and it was immediately clear that Taylor was going to get off. The 'double jeopardy' system meant that a man could not be tried more than twice for the same crime and that if the second trial was ruled as unsafe the accused would have to be dismissed. Hanna's quasi-humorous description of [a jury] 'running around in wee bits and pieces in Donaghadee and Antrim' was intended, successfully as it turned out, to blur the undoubted fact, emphasised by the Lord Chief Justice as he passed sentence, that Taylor had been found guilty of 'a brutal and callous murder upon not merely convincing but conclusive evidence'.

Taylor looked like a man who had nothing to fear, that whatever happened he would not hang. In this matter he seemed to have friends in the highest of places. The admonitions of the Lord Chief Justice were virtually ignored not only by Hanna, who was, after all, the defence counsel, but also by the appeal judges, Porter and Black. The *Londonderry Sentinel* of 21 January carried the story and gave the main news in the first sober paragraph:

> The Northern Ireland Court of Criminal Appeal yesterday quashed the conviction and sentence of death imposed on Robert Taylor, the twenty-one years' old painter, of Meadow Street, Belfast, for the murder of Mrs. Minnie McGowan, the wife of a Belfast publican, at her home in Ponsonby Avenue, Belfast, on Easter Saturday last, and ordered his immediate release.

The chief ground for appeal was that the jury had 'separated' on two occasions; as reported his Lordship continued: 'A slight and harmless deviation might not perhaps vitiate a trial but when there is a whole series of such deviations the accused person was entitled to complain that his trial had not been conducted according to the established and recognised principles of their legal procedure.' The rest of the seventy minutes was devoted to complicated argument about precedents and a blow-by-blow account of the two excursions made by the jurymen.

There is at least a *prima-facie* case that the authorities were determined that the sentence would never be carried out. Did they fear that a Protestant hanging for the murder of a Catholic might cause serious sectarian rioting? The behaviour of Taylor's supporters certainly gave cause for some concern as they crowded the courtrooms and thronged outside during all the hearings. The thirty years that followed might suggest that a determination not to inflame rival factions was judicious. Another possibility, though it is unlikely given the culture of the time, was that the elaborate devices employed were to demonstrate a detestation of capital punishment. Nevertheless, there was a scandalous lack of justice 'being seen to be done', a legal principle as sacred as double jeopardy or lack of jury 'separation'. The formal enunciation of the principle was first made by the lawyer Gordon Hewart on 9 November 1923 at the King's Bench Division:

> A long line of cases shows that it is not merely of some importance, but is of fundamental importance that justice should not only be done, but should manifestly and undoubtedly be seen to be done.

The judicial review by the voluble Porter and the virtually silent Black was offensive to the layperson and grossly demeaning to the victim. There was also an indication that not all the citizens of the state were equal before the law. The *Sentinel* story ended with a piece of bad news for Hanna:

> Mr. G.B. Hanna, K.C., leading counsel for appellant, applied for costs, pointing out that there had been a considerable outlay for the transcripts of the shorthand notes, and asked if there was any way of reimbursing him. Lord Justice Porter (after consulting Lord Justice Black) refused the application.

Taylor was smuggled out of a side door of Crumlin Road courthouse and made his way quietly home. His crowd of supporters made their way home via the foot of Ponsonby. There the rendering of 'The Sash' was interrupted by those who felt it necessary to jeer at the scene of the murder. The main Protestant papers, the *News Letter* and the *Belfast Telegraph*, seemed, in their coverage of the quashing of the sentence, to have forgotten the context of the celebrations. Taylor's return was described as if he were a hero coming back from a career of mighty deeds. It was his last hurrah. He virtually disappeared off the map. His release was reported in the *Derry Journal* of 23 January and the story ended with the unsatisfactorily vague words: 'He may emigrate.'

Taylor was seen with Lily at a registry office on 22 February. By now their child must have been born but there is no record of whether it was male or female or what became of it. Taylor tried in vain to sell his story to the *Daily Mail*. An attempt to emigrate to Australia came to nothing after he was refused entry. There have been plenty of rumours, not least that he died years ago in Canada, but the most likely story is that he went to ground in the jungle of Belfast and may still survive today, aged seventy-eight. As 'Robert the Painter', he passed for a time into the city's folklore, remembered with shoulder-shrugging acquiescence by nationalists and perhaps conveniently forgotten by the rest.

Minnie's husband, John McGowan, did not long survive her. After his death Kathleen sold both the Waldorf pub and her parents' house, and went to live in England. She had been called as prosecution witness by Curran, some thought unnecessarily since any evidence that she could give was simply confirmatory. She identified the grisly parade of weapons used in the assault: the bread-knife now bent and bloody, her mother's bloody dress, the pot that had held the boiling soup that Taylor had poured over his victim, and the broken lemonade bottle full of Easter water, that had been smashed against her head, which her mother had filled at Mass that morning. Curran clearly wanted her there to generate sympathy by her young and stricken appearance.

Hanna soared in his political career, as his talents undoubtedly promised, and became Minister of Home Affairs in 1952. Later on he fell foul of the Orange Order over controversial marches along the Longstone Road, near Annalong in County Down. He tried, like his predecessor, Brian Maginess, to be impartial, banning a walk through the strongly nationalist area. The outcry province-wide was so strong that in 1955 he had to rescind the original ban and permit the 'traditional' walk. He left Stormont a year later to become a County Court judge, perhaps for other reasons than disaffection with the loyal brethren. Before his elevation he and Curran would find themselves embroiled in the next murder to rock the peaceful province and apparently connive at another patent miscarriage of justice.

13
PATRICIA CURRAN

PATRICIA CURRAN WAS THE DAUGHTER of Lancelot Curran, one of the most significant names of the Northern Ireland legal establishment, and the ultimately frustrated prosecutor in the trial of 'Robert the Painter'. He served as member for Carrick in the Stormont Parliament from 1945 till 1949 and was the youngest Attorney General in the history of that assembly. He was Senior Crown Prosecutor for County Down, Parliamentary Secretary to the Minister of Finance and Chief Whip, and in 1949 was elevated to the High Court Bench.

He and his family lived in a house known as The Glen in Whiteabbey, County Antrim, on the north shore of Belfast Lough. The house was unattractive in appearance and lay at the end of a dark and winding drive. The Currans had two children, Desmond, a successful barrister, who was heavily involved in the movement known as Moral Rearmament, and nineteen-year-old Patricia, who was rather more wayward.

Moral Rearmament (MRA) was founded in 1938 by American evangelist Frank Buchman and proved popular in Northern Ireland. MRA converts were relentless in their search for new members. Anything that might counter the perceived post-war headlong decline in morality appealed to the strong Presbyterianism of east Ulster. Buchman produced many handbooks and entertained possible neophytes at weeklong 'information courses' in Switzerland. In the Cold War politics of the early 1950s MRA's anti-Communism had many supporters, seduced by American selling techniques applied subtly to apostolic enthusiasm.

Ironically the 'evils' that MRA tried to combat seemed to be personified by young Patricia. She had none of the public virtues that would have pleased her remote father and ultra-respectable mother; it is even possible that Doris, her mother, disapproved of her being an undergraduate at Queen's. Then, in the summer of 1952, she found 'unsuitable' employment as the driver of a builder's lorry. In the small town atmosphere of peripheral Belfast — Whiteabbey was essentially a village — the 'judge's daughter' had 'a name'. Small town prurience and social envy played its part in that judgement and when her body was found with many stab wounds beside the driveway to her house there was great shock but rather less surprise. The Very Rev John Mc Sparran PP VF, the local Catholic parish priest, spoke about the killing at Mass on the Sunday. He said that 'the parish had been sullied by a foul crime. The crime was murder and murder of a most brutal kind... The murder was all the more abhorrent in that it was perpetrated on a young innocent and decent girl. The sympathy of the entire community went out to Mr Justice Curran, his wife and family at their great loss. The Curran family was held in the highest esteem, especially because of their Christian way of life.'

In 1952 cars were only just becoming available again after the war though they were still luxury items. Most people were dependent on bicycles or on reasonably efficient public transport. Certainly Patricia used the buses of the semi-state body, the Ulster Transport Authority (UTA) that plied along the north shore of the lough and with afternoon lectures on those November days it was usually late when she made the six-mile journey home. On dark evenings she would phone from the gate-lodge to have someone in the house drive down to collect her.

On 12 November 1952 she left Smithfield station as usual on the 5pm bus but never returned home. It was dark enough that late autumn evening and a thick fine drizzle added to the general misery. None of the family was at home and it was thought that she might have asked some local acquaintance to walk her up the driveway. The police were contacted in the early hours when Judge Curran rang to ask whether any bus accident had taken place in Whiteabbey because Patricia, who had been on her usual bus, had not come home. Constable Rutherford was on duty and immediately offered to come to The Glen to help with the search but Curran told him that it would not be necessary. (The constable knew how to behave with a high-court judge.) Five minutes later Constable Rutherford was surprised to receive a call from Doris Curran, unwittingly contradicting her husband's instructions. He arrived at the house at about 2am when Patricia's body was discovered by her father and brother. The family solicitor, Malcolm Davison, whom Curran rang before speaking to Constable Rutherford, helped them to load the already stiffening body into his car. They took Patricia to the family doctor, Kenneth Wilson, reaching his surgery at 2.20am. His initial estimate of the time of death was sometime between 11pm and midnight and because of the number of wounds suffered he ventured the opinion that death had been caused by a shotgun.

The body was positioned just off the driveway and there was little or no blood on the ground, a few drops at most. Her files and textbooks were placed neatly by her side as were a glove, a Juliet cap, two scarves and a handbag. Despite the wet evening they were all dry and, according to witnesses, Patricia had none of these belongings with her on the bus. To say it was improper for a judge, a solicitor and a serving member of the RUC to have risked the destruction of forensic evidence at the crime scene is a rank understatement — it verged on the criminal. The girl's body was sufficiently advanced in rigor mortis to make her easy to lift but it was necessary to have her feet pushed out of the open window of Malcolm Davison's car while Desmond cradled her body in the back seat. He insisted that he heard her breathe but it was simply exhalation of air from the lungs. This provided the best excuse for the wanton bad practice at the scene.

The body was covered in blood which gave it the appearance of shotgun trauma, and it wasn't until a proper pathological examination was carried out by Dr Morrell at 5am that the true cause of the wounds was discovered. In fact the weapon used was a knife and there were a total of thirty-seven stab wounds located on face, neck, legs and chest. Her heart had been pierced twice and both leg-arteries were severed.

What was certainly clear from the beginning was that Patricia had been killed elsewhere and then placed beside the driveway. However, there was no indication of dragging, either on the ground or on Patricia's clothing. Family involvement seemed likely but the judge refused to allow his clan be questioned until four days after the murder, and it would be another three days before police were allowed to examine the house. When the fall guy was finally brought to trial his defence team, Basil Kelly and HA McVeigh, only accepted the brief on the condition that they wouldn't have to question any member of the Curran family — which would have been career suicide.

The avoidance of proper procedure was facilitated by the fact that the judge who finally heard the case, Lord Chief MacDermott, was a family friend of the Currans, as was the Inspector-General of the RUC, Sir Richard Pim, who in turn was an intimate of Prime Minister Winston Churchill. The RUC continued their examination of the unpreserved scene, finding no satisfactory explanation for the inconsistencies in the case. They used highly sensitive metal detectors but nothing was found.

The investigation continued with great intensity. All undergraduates at Queen's with even the slightest acquaintance with Patricia were interviewed by the police. Between the time of the murder and the following January 40,000 people were questioned and 9,000 of these provided written statements. Early that spring, while hitching back from Dundalk to Belfast, I was given a lift by two guards who, upon reaching their station at the border, courteously but firmly insisted that I come in with them after they discovered I was a Queen's postgraduate student. There followed a fairly searching interrogation and I was asked about Patricia Curran.

Unusually, indeed against all practice, senior detectives from Scotland Yard were imported on the instructions of Sir Richard Pim. Superintendent John Capstick was the leading murder specialist in the Yard. His name was known to the general public, especially to those who read the many broadsheet Sundays in that post-war golden age of newspapers. He brought his assistant, Sergeant Dennis Hawkins, and they went to work assiduously. They had many inconsistencies to reconcile and questions to answer: where and when was the crime committed? Why had the body been carried to the place where it was found? Who had inflicted such frenzied injuries on the victim? She was last seen at 5.20pm by Roy Patterson, a Whiteabbey neighbour, who had travelled on the same bus. From the level of rigor when the body was found the time of death should have been around 11pm, leaving five and a half hours unaccounted for.

The usual suspects — intimates, boyfriends, neighbours — did not seem culpable. The nearest thing to a boyfriend was John Steel, with whom she had spent the afternoon in a teashop. He had seen her off on the 5pm bus from Smithfield that afternoon but could not otherwise be linked to her death. The usual pleas for information were made. Judge Curran made his bid for information: 'We plead with everyone who has the slightest piece of information that might help, to give such information to the police. We are concerned to see that this foul murderer is brought to justice, not through any spirit of vengeance, but to ensure that other people's daughters may be safe. We keep asking ourselves who will be the next victim.' The pleas were not especially successful. The murder weapon, thought to be a two-edged stiletto, was never found in spite of meticulous searching. Nor were the missing hands, winder and glass of Patricia's watch that had been refastened to her wrist with the face turned inwards ever discovered. The absolute lack of progress was beginning to have its effect on the investigators' morale. Shreds of information, however trivial, were seized upon.

George Chambers, an eleven-year-old newspaper delivery boy, was persuaded to go to the police and tell them that he had been in the Curran driveway at around 5.30pm. On his way back from the postbox he fancied that he heard something in the shrubbery which frightened him and caused him to run down the lane to the main Whiteabbey Road. He saw nothing, however, and did not notice any books or clothing beside the path. An ostensibly more useful piece of information came eight days after the murder when local woman Hettie Lyttle said that she had seen a man come out of the gates of The Glen around 6.00pm. She described him as being pale, tall and wearing a wide-brimmed hat. The police issued a press statement indicating that they wished to interview a man 'aged about thirty, height about six foot, thin build, noticeably old scar on the left side of his face and mouth. Seen wearing a soft hat of American type with a wide brim and may be wearing either a fawn raincoat or a grey herringbone overcoat.' Mrs Lyttle had not been able to identify the man she saw in any of the police photographs and may well have been prompted by her interviewers to supplement her original description. No person answering this description was ever found and a reward of £1,000 offered on 1 January 1953 was never claimed.

The sphere of enquiries of Capstick and Hawkins was eventually widened to include the RAF station at Edenmore, which was a short distance from the Curran house. When news of the murder reached the camp an internal investigation was begun immediately. The twenty-two national servicemen were interrogated by the OC, Wing-Commander Richard Popple, and each accounted successfully for his movements between 11pm and midnight on the twelfth. When the investigators began to suggest an earlier time for the occurrence and enquired about alibis for the hours between 5 and 6pm they found that two airmen were alone that evening, AC2 Ian Hay Gordon and Corporal Henry Connor. The two reacted instinctively and gave each other alibis, saying that they were together during that time. Gordon was unique among other ranks in that he had been invited to dinner at The Glen by Desmond, Patricia's brother.

Ian Hay Gordon was twenty, a year older than Patricia Curran, and miles apart from her in intelligence and social class. The 'Hay' part of the name was an old Scots nickname meaning 'tall', singularly inappropriate in his case. He was shy, awkward socially and physically, and easily guyed by his fellow national servicemen. Some smarter companions persuaded him, for example, that he had to use L-plates on his bicycle as he rode about the camp. He was alleged to be homosexual, though showing very little evidence of sexual drive. He came from Dollar, between the firths of Tay and Forth on the east coast of Scotland, where the prevailing religious practice was Presbyterian. He continued to attend Presbyterian services when stationed at Edenmore and formed a slight acquaintance with the Rev SJ Wylie, the minister of Whiteabbey, who acted as camp chaplain. It was at one of these services that he met Desmond Curran, who was a fervent churchgoer. The messianic instinct that was a part of Moral Rearmament practice suggested to Curran that Gordon was an appropriate person to cultivate. They met fairly regularly after the Sunday meeting and at the Presbyterian student hostel in Howard Street, in Belfast city centre. He then invited Gordon to dinner in The Glen, which was a foolish if not an actually cruel thing to do, imposing severe strain on the awkward and not especially bright AC2. When Gordon arrived at the house Judge Curran lowered his evening paper for a moment and returned to it without comment; Doris Curran was uneasy and inhospitable. Only Patricia made any attempt to show him kindness and make him feel at ease. It was the only contact he had with his supposed victim.

Capstick and Hawkins had a responsibility, not necessarily to find the truth, but certainly to finish the case. They began an intensive interrogation of the unfortunate young man. He had no counsel; there should at least have been an RAF officer present, though the police claimed that the lack of a 'soldier's friend' was at the request of Gordon. (The phrase comes from military court-martial practice.) The questioning was more intensive on the second day and lasted from 9am to 7.45pm. Gordon's disorientation and mental confusion increased. He remembered feeling very drowsy, wondering if his coffee might have been drugged. The strongest lever that Capstick had was Gordon's friendship with Wesley Courtenay, a local homosexual known to the police. It must be remembered that homosexual acts were criminal with a mandatory prison sentence. Gordon was not so much worried about any penalties but he was desperate that his mother should not get to hear about his proclivities. Eventually he decided that if he cooperated with his interrogators that he would be released. At this stage he would have admitted anything. His confession is a very webby document, filled with gaps, generally incoherent and clearly suggested to him if not actually dictated. This was the main part of the confession:

> I left the camp at Edenmore shortly after 4.00pm on Wednesday afternoon, November 12, 1952 to deliver the mail to Whiteabbey P.O. I was there from five to ten minutes, then went to Montgomery's paper shop in the main street to collect the camp newspapers. I would not have been very long there. I believe I called in at the bookies, approximately opposite Quiery's but off the main road. I placed a bet there on a horse for one of the airmen in the camp, I forget his name. I think I then went back to the camp with the newspapers. I probably had my tea about 5.00pm. It took me about five minutes for my tea. I think I then changed into my civilian wear of sports coat and flannels. I then walked back alone to Whiteabbey and met Patricia Curran between The Glen and Whiteabbey

Post Office. She said to me, 'Hello, Ian,' or something like that. I said, 'Hello, Patricia.' We had a short general conversation. I forget what we talked about but she asked me to escort her to her home up The Glen. I agreed to do so, because it was nearly dark and there was none of the family at the gate to The Glen. I can understand anyone being afraid of going up The Glen in the dark, because the light is completely cut out because the trees meet at the top. I noticed that Patricia was carrying a handbag and something else, I just forget what it was. It appeared to be wrapped up, whatever it was, books or something. She was wearing a yellow hat. It was just about The Glen entrance where she first spoke to me. We both walked up The Glen together and I think I was on her left hand side. After we walked for a few yards I either held her left hand or arm as we walked along. She did not object and was quite cheerful. We carried on walking up The Glen until we came to the spot where the street lamps' light does not reach. It was quite dark there and I said to Patricia, 'Do you mind if I kiss you?' or words to that effect. We stopped walking and stood on the grass verge on the left hand side of the drive. She laid her things on the grass and I think she laid her hat there as well. Before she did this she was not keen on me giving her a kiss, but consented in the end. I kissed her once or twice to begin with and she did not object. She then asked me to continue escorting her up the drive. I did not do so as I found I could not stop kissing her. As I was kissing her, I let my hand slip down her body between her coat and her clothes. Her coat was open and my hand may have touched her breast, but I'm not sure. She struggled and said, 'Don't, don't, you beast,' or something like that. I struggled with her and she said to me: 'Let me go or I will tell my father.' I then lost control of myself and Patricia fell on the grass sobbing. She appeared to have fainted, because she went limp. I am a bit hazy about what happened next but I probably pulled the body of Patricia through the bushes to hide it. I dragged her by her arms or hands, but I cannot remember. Even before this happened I do not think I was capable of knowing what I was doing. I was confused at the time and believe I stabbed her once or twice with my service knife. I had been carrying this in my trouser pocket. I am not quite sure what kind of knife it was. I may have caught her by the throat to stop her from shouting. I may have pushed her scarves against her mouth to stop her shouting. It is all very hazy to me, but I think I was disturbed either by seeing a light or hearing footsteps in the drive. I must have remained hidden and later walked out of The Glen at the gate lodge on to the main road. As far as I know I crossed the road and threw the knife into the sea. I felt that something awful must have happened and quickly walked back to the camp. I went to my billet and arrived there at roughly 6.30pm. There was no one in the billet at the time and I saw I had some patches of Patricia's blood on my flannels. I took a fairly large wooden nailbrush from my kit. I got some water and soap from the ablutions and scrubbed the blood off my flannels. I must have done this but I do not quite remember. As far as I know no person saw me doing it. I then went to our Central Registry and did some typing as I was preparing for an examination. I went to bed at between 9.30pm and 10.00pm. I got up roughly at about 7.00am on Thursday, November 13, 1952. I had my breakfast and did my routine duties. At between 8.15am and 8.30am that day the postman was delivering mail to our camp, and he told me that Mr Justice Curran's daughter had been found dead in the grounds. He may have said she had been shot. I just cannot remember...

It is an interesting piece of fabrication full of doubts and showing no real awareness of the facts. The dreamlike air of the narrative would help persuade the jury that Gordon was not fully *compos mentis*; with the death sentence still in existence a verdict of guilty but insane would save Gordon's life. If Gordon had been represented properly the 'confession' would not have been admitted as evidence. He withdrew it immediately, explaining to his reluctant defence team that he had been harangued by four policemen for days, ten hours at a stretch. Nevertheless Lord Chief Justice MacDermott, the presiding judge, permitted the fabricated document to be heard as evidence. Any chance Gordon might have had of rebuttal, of explaining to the jury the conditions under which he had agreed to sign, were denied him. He was not put in the witness box and the jury had to accept his confession as authentic. They also heard AR Lewis, a leading Harley Street psychiatrist, give as his professional opinion that Gordon was not sane. He opined that Gordon was 'very childish', which was a considerable overstatement to describe a perhaps immature personality. The other terms used in Lewis' evidence were grossly inaccurate: 'abnormal personality', 'schizoid person', 'inadequate psychopath'. His motive may have been to save an unfortunate wretch from the gallows. Lewis's professional opinion, no doubt given with all the authority and confidence of the expert, complemented Gordon's signed confession, convincing the jury that Gordon was the murderer despite the lack of forensic evidence; clothes without blood or hair, no trace of earth or vegetable mould. There was absolutely no proof beyond a forced and repudiated confession. They found him guilty but insane and he was committed to Holywell Mental Institute.

Here he soon became a 'trusty' and was free to walk out the open gate at any time, as was appropriate since he was perfectly sane. The medical superintendent, Gilbert Smith, examined him frequently and never saw a trace of mental abnormality. His reports that Gordon was 'not of unsound mind' were countermanded annually by a Ministry of Health inspector who continued to describe him as having 'schizoid tendencies', therefore requiring Gordon to continue at Holywell where 'he was receiving treatment appropriate to his condition'. In his acquiescent way Gordon made no attempt to leave until a kind of release in August 1960, after almost eight years in confinement. Brian Faulkner, then Minister of Home Affairs, had him virtually smuggled out of the country booking him on to a plane to Glasgow as John Cameron. This was a necessary condition of his freedom and he lived in a state of personality occlusion until a judicial review in 2000 exonerated him from all charges. He lived quietly in Glasgow working for a time as a packer in the famous printing and publishing house of William Collins. It was reported that he continued to suffer nightmares about his confinement.

The court of appeal's quashing of the case established that the evidence produced by the prosecution (and more or less accepted by the defence) at the original trial was flawed; important exculpatory evidence had been suppressed. For example James Spence, one of Gordon's fellow national servicemen, told the police that he had seen Gordon in the NAAFI at 6pm, showing no signs of having committed a murder at 5.45pm. A successful legal appeal does not prove absolute innocence; it merely affirms that no reliable evidence was brought to establish guilt. There does, however, appear to be moral certainty about Gordon's absolute innocence. He suffered collateral damage, to use a term of modern warfare, by an unfortunate peripheral association with what seems to have been a spectacularly dysfunctional family. We will never know what happened on the night of 12 November 1952 and speculation is pointless. Did Patricia see something she shouldn't and had to be silenced? Did a murderous rage overcome some member of the family that resulted in her death? Did she perhaps tell her mother that she was pregnant and suffered the dire consequences?

The Curran case continued to fascinate criminologists, both professional and amateur. Such a one was Sir Ludovic Kennedy, whose book *10 Rillington Place* described how Timothy Evans, a man of limited intelligence, was hanged for crimes committed by the savvy John Reginald Halliday Christie. His 1970 television documentary about the Curran case was suppressed by the Stormont government led by James Chichester-Clark. Duncan Webb, a relentless populist journalist, had been fascinated by the Curran case for years. He got to examine The Glen in 1984, after Judge Curran's death, and found a large stain in one of the upstairs rooms which he believed could be blood and most likely belonging to Patricia Curran. Unfortunately he died before he was able to write his conclusion to the mystery of the judge's daughter. Since DNA matching wasn't yet available no final proof could be found but Webb's findings confirmed the popular opinion that the murder was an inside job. The Glen no longer exists and the house was destroyed, preventing further forensic examination.

The only surviving member of the family is Desmond, now a Roman Catholic priest with a mission station at Khayelitsha in South Africa, whose work among the dispossessed is exemplary. When interviewed in January 1995 for a BBC documentary, *More Sinned Against Than Sinning*, he insisted that the family were not involved in Patricia's murder and that Gordon was guilty. He converted to Catholicism after his sister's death and was, consequently, barred from the family home. Five years later he was ordained in Rome and has since continued his missionary work in South Africa.

The difficulties associated with investigation of the case had no deleterious effect on Judge Curran's legal career. He became Lord Justice of Appeal in 1956 and was knighted in 1964. His demeanour continued to seem remote and aloof, though he surprised everyone by accepting Desmond's invitation to his ordination, perhaps in an act of atonement. It was certainly a bold decision that earlier in his career would have been injudicious. By then he remained so austerely uncommunicative that no one questioned him about his reason for assenting to a piece of popery, as it was no doubt described. Until his death in 1984 he was noted for this almost inert inaccessibility. Doris, his wife, never quite recovered from the events of that November night and became a recluse, dying in 1975.

As a final statement on the affair I take the liberty of quoting from the RUC County Inspector Kennedy's report, not mentioned at Gordon's trial. Kennedy had successfully led the investigation until the introduction of the egregious Capstick.

> It was decided to pursue every line of enquiry before allowing our thoughts to concentrate on something which seemed too fantastic to believe, namely that the Currans were covering up the murder and telling a tissue of lies.

Now fifty-four years later the story of the Curran tragedy continues to fascinate. Above all the photographs taken of Ian Hay Gordon at the time of his trial in January 1953 and then in 2000, when his name was finally cleared, are a reminder of a blatant miscarriage of justice and of a time when the standard of legal procedure in Northern Ireland was less than honourable.

14
PENNY McALLISTER

DRUMKEERAGH FOREST PARK is in County Down at the foot of Slieve Croob, the source of Belfast's river Lagan. The nearest town is Ballynahinch which is about four miles to the northeast. It was in this beautiful and lonely place on 27 March 1991 that two women went for a walk with pet dogs, Monty and Barton. Susan Christie was a private in the Ulster Defence Regiment (UDR) and Penny was the civilian wife of Captain Duncan McAllister, of the Royal Corps of Signals. The women soldiers in the UDR were known as 'Greenfinches' and Christie was a well-known if not necessarily popular Greenfinch. The park was laid out in trails that led right round the forest and after the women did one round of the outer three mile circuit they agreed to go round again. Sometime later Christie was seen by Eileen Rice, making her way to the car park with the two dogs. Mrs Rice had gone with her husband and two children to have a picnic in the forest because the spring weather was so pleasant. Susan's manner was strange and her progress uncertain. She babbled incoherently about an attack by a man in the forest and pleaded with the woman to 'help Penny'.

Mr Rice went as fast as he could for the police while his wife tried to comfort Susan. The Rices eventually took her to a house nearby and there they waited for the police and an ambulance. Patrick McGrath, a local doctor, was sent for and he examined the distraught woman. He found that her underwear was torn, and her hands were covered with blood though there was only a small wound on her left thigh. The ambulance took her to Downe Hospital in Downpatrick where she repeated her story that a wild bearded man had jumped out of the undergrowth and attacked them with a large knife. He lunged at Penny but Susan managed to escape. It was left to Captain McAllister's senior officer, Major Andrew Johnstone, to break the news to him about his wife's death.

McAllister had only spoken to Penny a few hours earlier; she was busy cleaning their house for her parents' visit before going to pick them up at Belfast's main airport at Aldergrove in County Antrim. McAllister's grief was interrupted by the realisation that Penny's parents, Norma and Desmond Squire, would be at Aldergrove at 6pm. McAllister had already phoned his own parents and had given way to a howling grief. An army helicopter flew him and Major Johnstone to the airport where he broke the news to his in-laws in a small room near the baggage carousel. As sorrow overwhelmed him again he did his best to comfort the stricken couple. They returned home the next day to Ashton Keynes, a pretty little village in Wiltshire, to make preparations for Penny's funeral. Her body was eventually flown out and she was buried in the dress in which she had been married six years before.

Drumkeeragh Forest was searched by two battalions of soldiers and surveyed by a helicopter but there was no trace of any stranger. However, a knife, which was forensically proven to be the murder weapon, was found 260 yards from the body. Susan Christie described how she had stopped to tie her lace and when she looked up she saw a man bending over Penny's body. He turned towards her and might have killed her too but one of the dogs began barking and, much more effectively, she kneed the stranger in the testicles. Though not trained in unarmed combat and self-defence, Christie was a vigorous, observant twenty-three-year-old and she knew the basics.

As the police investigation continued Christie gradually became conscious of a change of attitude. She felt that she was no longer being treated as a plucky survivor who had lost her friend. Dr McGrath had voiced his suspicions to the police that her injuries may have been self-inflicted. She was subject to more intensive questioning and began to show signs that the experienced interrogation team could identify.

Four days after the murder Captain McAllister rang the incident room at Ballynahinch and asked to speak to one of the detectives. They arranged to meet at Gough military barracks in Armagh where McAllister confessed that he had been having an affair with Susan Christie. In spite of being happily married McAllister embarked on the risky affair in the spring of 1990 when Christie joined the sub-aqua diving club he set up. The young private was obviously attracted to the captain and blatantly flirted with him, unworried by the gossip that inevitably followed such an obvious campaign of seduction.

By early summer McAllister found himself relishing the flirting and began to respond in kind. During a diving expedition the two were temporarily alone on the boat while the others explored an old wreck. McAllister made no bones about his attraction but warned Christie that an affair would have to be secret as it could destroy their careers. He also emphasised that the attraction was purely physical and likely to be of short duration. Most importantly he told her that he had no intention of leaving Penny whom he loved dearly. Christie seemed to accept these ground rules and the couple consummated the 'relationship' the following Saturday when Penny decided to forgo diving for shopping.

From a practical point of view there were several inconveniences. Since the McAllisters had no children Penny was free to accompany Duncan to all non-military events, thereby leaving little time for Susan. The other difficulty was the disparity in their ranks. McAllister was a commissioned officer in the regular army while Christie was a private in the UDR and the twain was not encouraged to meet except in the line of duty.

The ancient Greeks regarded lust as a kind of madness and this certainly seemed true in McAllister's case. He loved his wife but could not resist Christie and took ridiculous risks to be with her. He continually emphasised the need for secrecy but when Christie asked him to meet her outside of club activities he agreed. On 13 July 1990 they even had a picnic beside Lowry's Lake, one mile from the camp on the road to Hamilton's Bawn.

Christie's temperament was not ideal for the concealment of an illicit affair. She had a wilful streak and liked to be the centre of attraction. She realised that her passion for McAllister was turning into possessive love which wasn't reciprocated. He continued to warn her that he would never leave Penny and that if she ever found out about their affair he would end it immediately. That autumn Penny found that she was pregnant. She kept the news to herself because she had begun to suspect a more serious aspect to Christie's obvious crush on her husband, that they actually were having an affair. Penny refused to use the pregnancy to make Duncan leave Christie; she preferred that he come to his senses and end the relationship of his own volition. She did not realise the passion that the Greenfinch felt for Duncan nor the lengths to which she was prepared go to have him.

The diving club arranged a trip to Ascension Island in October 1990. The volcanic island lies in the South Atlantic, 1,100 miles northwest of St Helena, and its warm, clear waters made it ideally suited for diving. For a while it looked as if Penny could not go since she was not army personnel and the plane fare, at £1,500, would have been prohibitive. Christie was delighted until McAllister made one more attempt, pleading with the Ministry of Defence to make Penny a compassionate case. This time he was successful; she could travel at a cost of £450 for the return fare. Christie accused McAllister of preferring Penny, who she was intensely jealous of, to her.

The flight from Brize Norton, in Oxfordshire (an airfield which had figured heavily in the Falklands campaign eight years before) took nine hours. During that time McAllister roved about the plane chatting to all his passengers and was noticeably spending a lot of time talking to Christie. Perhaps by now he felt it judicious to keep her sweet. She refused to eat her first meal on Ascension, saying she wasn't hungry. It was Penny who had cooked it and McAllister assumed that her lack of appetite was part of her anti-Penny campaign. She brightened up considerably when the Ascension diving club held a party for the visitors and she made herself the centre of attraction, although her possessiveness with McAllister alarmed the group and was made pretty plain to Penny. McAllister was becoming more and more determined to bring the destructive business to a close. After the trip he attempted to end the affair but Christie made the usual scene and successfully seduced him again.

On 2 November McAllister was startled by a phone call from Christie saying she was pregnant. They met later to discuss the situation. There were three options: she could have an abortion, she could have the baby and not reveal the father's name, or she could make the affair public. McAllister preferred the first option; after the operation life would continue as before, both would keep their jobs and no one need find out. Christie eventually agreed to have her pregnancy terminated with much emotional words about 'killing the baby'. Until the abortion could be performed McAllister felt he had to continue with the relationship. It was with some pained relief that he then heard she was in hospital after suffering a miscarriage.

Christie was an intelligent manipulator and a brilliant liar. One wonders now just how genuine the pregnancy was. Her return to health was swift but she was enraged when she heard that Penny had had a miscarriage as well. Meanwhile McAllister was deeply shocked as he hadn't known that his wife was even pregnant. He suddenly realised just how badly he had treated Penny and resolved to find some means of extrication without causing too much hurt to Christie.

A possible opportunity presented itself in the New Year. Christie was very ambitious. Her second dearest wish was to become a commissioned officer but she lacked an O-level pass in mathematics. She would have to go to Beaconsfield in

Buckinghamshire for an intensive three month course from April to the end of June. McAllister determined to make the break well before April but then continued to see Christie as winter turned to spring. Andrew Johnstone, his major, informed him that he was due for promotion either in Ireland or in Germany. When Penny heard she urged him to stay where he was, assuming that was what he wanted. In fact he was happy to go to Germany. Penny had lived there for much of her girlhood and they had met in Lippstadt.

Christie begged him not to rashly break off their relationship and, with a convincing appearance of contrition, began to make peace offerings to the agreeable Penny. The walk through Drumkeeragh was part of this reconciliation. During the second circuit of the forest, at the point farthest from the car park, Christie, who was wearing gloves in spite of the mild day, told Penny to walk ahead while she tied her shoelace. Penny did so and Christie, taking a butcher's knife from the pocket of her tracksuit, imitated the simulated attack she had seen in her unarmed combat classes. She jerked Penny's head back with a lift of her left arm and slashed her throat, pulling the deeply imbedded knife towards her right ear. Penny died almost immediately. Christie stabbed herself lightly in the left thigh and ripped her underwear.

Once McAllister made his confession to the RUC, Christie became the chief suspect. It was interesting how the press reporting of the case changed about the same time. In the *News Letter* of Thursday, 28 March, the day after the murder, the headline read 'Stake-out in forest of death.' The story began:

> Police and soldiers are hunting a psychopathic murderer who knifed an Army captain's wife to death in a remote forest yesterday. The assassin cut the throat of his victim near Ballynahinch, Co Down, stabbed her to death and then tried unsuccessfully to kill her friend who was later described as 'comfortable' in hospital.

Friday's paper advised, '"Psycho" still on the run', and had a picture of two policemen with tracker dogs in Drumkeeragh. By 1 June a 40-point headline screamed 'Murder in the forest denied' with a sub-head 'But UDR woman admits killing.'

The detectives informed Christie that McAllister had told them about their affair. At first she stormed and blustered, denying everything but then, with a change of tactics, she insisted that McAllister and Penny had an 'open marriage', so Penny didn't mind about her husband's affair. She also claimed that Penny had had many affairs with both officers and men. It did not take long for the police to confirm that she was lying. Christie changed her story again, saying that her mind was a complete blank about the death of Penny. All she could remember was seeing Penny lying on the ground spurting blood from the wound in her throat but she could not have been responsible because 'I would never do anything like that to Penny.' She maintained this position throughout her trial at Downpatrick court and never varied it.

The hearing began on Monday, 1 June 1992, more than fifteen months after Penny's death and nearly two years from the beginning of the affair. When asked to plead she said she was not guilty of murder but admitted to manslaughter. The press, especially the British redtops, dubbed the Drumkeeragh tragedy as 'The Fatal Attraction Killing', though the parallels were far from true. John Creaney QC, who led for the Crown, said that Christie's obsessive jealousy drove her to see Penny as an obstacle that must be removed.

On 3 June McAllister stood in the witness box and rarely looked near the dock where his mistress sat, her eyes full of tears. The details of the affair were examined in some embarrassing detail by Peter Smyth QC, Christie's lawyer, who referred to the disparity of their military ranks and the possibility that he created expectations in Christie's mind that he had no intention of fulfilling. McAllister insisted that he had always made it clear that their relationship was an affair, based on mutual physical attraction, and little if anything else. Pressed relentlessly by Smyth he finally admitted that he did tell Christie that he loved her.

The question of Christie's claim to being pregnant and of her apparently fortuitous miscarriage resulted in possibly the most insistent and embarrassing cross-questioning that McAllister had to endure. The three options were listed and McAllister's responses analysed. What weakened his position and diminished him as an honourable man at the mercy of his own passions, was his constant returning to Christie. Smyth seemed to be suggesting complicity or, if not, suggesting that Christie felt he could be made complicit. One thing she took for granted was that he would welcome the death of Penny so that he could be free with her. Smyth tried to establish that a few days before Drumkeeragh Christie was in a highly emotional state at the prospect of the McAllisters going to Germany while she went to Sandhurst to commence officer training. He seemed to have succeeded in persuading the jury (and Lord Justice Kelly) that Christie was desperate, that she had been treated abominably and misled by a heartless McAllister.

It was on 8 June, a week after the trial began, when Susan Christie left the dock and climbed into the witness stand. The court was crowded with sightseers and the press. She described their first meeting when she first joined the sub-aqua club and of their mutual passion. She insisted that he had often told her that he loved her, and not as a friend or a willing sexual partner as he had insisted to the court. She added that after her miscarriage they continued to make love. She found it difficult to get McAllister to talk about their future. She was in a highly emotional state on 16 March , saying that she thought Penny had tried to kill her during a dive. She then admitted in the witness box that this was not true. Smyth led her to discuss the actual murder. He pressed her to respond to the accusation that she had killed Penny. She replied, 'I accept it,' but claimed that she remembered nothing of the actual deed and maintained that position throughout the trial and after.

Evidence of her mental state was given by forensic psychiatrist William Anderson Norris. He had studied her case thoroughly and examined her twice while she was in Maghaberry prison. His opinion was that her depression was mild and she was pretending that she didn't remember the details of the killing. In his summing-up Lord Justice Kelly seemed to favour the defence. He suggested a series of tragedies: the cruel death of Penny and the misery that had inflicted on her husband, family and friends. He suggested that Christie was also a tragic figure and that, at the time of the killing, could have been in a condition of diminished responsibility. He told the jury that if they accepted the evidence of the psychiatrists for the defence they should find Christie guilty of manslaughter. If they accepted the prosecution's psychiatrists' evidence the proper verdict would be murder. The Crown refused to accept a plea of diminished responsibility but the burden of the summing-up was for a mental state in which she was not herself.

After three and a half hours the jury returned saying they could not reach a unanimous verdict. The judge replied that he would accept a majority one and, thirty minutes later, they returned a not guilty verdict. The judge imposed a sentence of five years imprisonment which caused uproar in the courtroom — Christie would be free after eighteen months. There was a storm of protest in Britain as well as Northern Ireland. The *Sunday Life*'s reporter expressed what was in everybody's mind:

> If it is the case that a young and attractive woman can lose her life so brutally through absolutely no fault of her own, and that her killer can be freed in so short a time as Susan Christie, then we are entitled to ask: does the punishment fit the crime?

The piece concluded with the sentence: 'There appears a deep gulf between the public perception of the Susan Christie case and the judge's verdict.'

It was too much. The Attorney-General's office examined the

case and asked the Court of Appeal to review the sentence. The three appeal judges gave their opinions in November 1992. The senior judge, Lord Chief Justice Sir Brian Hutton, concluded that Christie had a very considerable degree of residual responsibility for the killing that made a sentence of five years unduly lenient. He told her that, by a majority decision, he and his colleagues intended to increase the length of her sentence from five to nine years. The second appeal judge, Lord Justice Murray, considered that the planning and the premeditation of the crime, the purchase and sharpening of the murder weapon and her attempt at a cover-up, the complete absence of mental illness and the advantage to her of removing her rival were all fairly clear pointers of residual responsibility for the crime. The third judge of appeal, Lord Justice MacDermott, dissented, saying that he found Lord Justice Kelly's sentence to be appropriate, combining leniency and mercy. Christie was released in December 1995, having with full remission served nearly five years. McAllister never visited her in prison and she was dishonourably discharged from the army.

The case was referred to in an article on 12 November 1999 in the *Irish Examiner* by Terry Prone called 'Getting Away with Murder':

> Less than 10 years ago, Penny McAllister's body was found in a forest in County Down. Her throat had been cut with such venomous force, the head was almost severed.
>
> Susan Christie, in her early 20s, was convicted of killing the wife of her lover. She served four and a half years for a crime so vicious that, 30 years ago, would have ensured hanging if a man had done it. Instead, before her 30th birthday, she was free, had a new identity and was 'getting on with the rest of her life'.
>
> Susan Christie's extreme violence to get what she wanted may not be the rule but it isn't the exception any more.

SELECT BIBLIOGRAPHY

Anon. *Some Authentic Particulars of the Life of John Macnaughton, Esq of Benvarden*. London: 1762

Baker, Joe (ed.) *Belfast Murders*. Belfast: 1994–6

Bardon, Jonathan. *A History of Ulster*. Belfast: 1992

Belfast Evening Telegraph

Belfast News Letter

Davies, Nicholas. *A Deadly Kind of Love*. London: 1994

Dolan, Liam. *The Third Earl of Leitrim*. Letterkenny: 1978

Irish News & Belfast Morning News

Kiely, David M. *Bloody Women*. Dublin: 1999

Londonderry/Derry Journal

Londonderry Sentinel

Londonderry/Derry Standard

McAlindon, Tom. *Bloodstains in Ulster*. Dublin: 2006

McNamee, Eoin. *Blue Tango*. London: 2001

Richards, AR. *Irish Murders*. New Lanark: 2001

(Ed.) Sweeney, Frank. *Hanging Crimes*. Cork: 2005

Sweeney, Frank. *The Murder of Conell Boyle, County Donegal, 1898*. Dublin: 2002.

Victorian Ulster Murders. Belfast:1994